WHEN DINOSAURS RULED THE EARTH

by David Norman

DORSET PRESS
NEW YORK

Credits

Author: David Norman, B.Sc., Ph.D., F.L.S., Department of Zoology and University Museum, Oxford
Scientific Consultant: Alan Charig, M.A., Ph.D., M.I.Biol.
Illustrator: John Sibbick
Editor: Trisha Costick
Art Editors: John Curnoe, Edward Pitcher
Production: Richard Churchill
Diagram Artists: Tom Stimpson pp. 8–9, 12–13, 20–21; John Brock pp. 37, 74–75; John Curnoe maps and scale diagrams

This edition published by Dorset Press, a division of Marboro Books Corp.

Produced by Marshall Cavendish Books Limited, 58 Old Compton Street, London W1V 5PA

© Marshall Cavendish Limited 1985
This impression 1990

ISBN 0 88029 509 0
Printed and bound in Portugal

Introduction

The last dinosaurs walked this Earth 64 million years ago—an almost unimaginably long time. They were members of a great group of reptiles that had dominated the Earth for 140 million years. Yet because the remains of these long-dead animals have been preserved as fossils it has proved possible, by painstaking work of excavation and scientific study, to learn much about their anatomy, way of life and evolutionary history—in fact to almost bring them back to life.

The purpose of this book is to introduce the enthusiast to most of the better-known dinosaurs. This is done by combining accurate life-like colour illustrations with careful discussion of what is presently known about dinosaur biology. In this way the reader should learn a great deal, not only about individual dinosaurs, but also of the world they inhabited and their position in the much greater history of life on Earth.

Contents

Reconstructing a dinosaur

All the prehistoric animals described and illustrated in this book are known only from their fossilized remains (see pages 8–9). Unfortunately these fossils do not give us a complete picture of the living animal to which they belonged. The fossils we find may be bones, shells or merely faint impressions left on the surface of rocks. After all, we cannot expect to find the soft parts, such as the skin, muscles and nerves, which rot away very quickly after an animal dies (unless, as in some very exceptional circumstances, the carcass of the dead animal dries out and then

Below: The largest mounted dinosaur skeleton in the world is this *Brachiosaurus* in the Museum of Natural Science in East Berlin. Its head alone reaches a height of nearly 13 metres (43 feet).

becomes mummified before burial). Obviously this presents problems if we wish to make accurate life-like restorations of these long-dead animals.

If we are lucky enough to find all the fossilized bones of one of these animals, we can soon start to reconstruct its skeleton.

First we must find out what sort of animal it was. To do this, specialists must study the bones very carefully, looking for tell-tale clues. For instance, if the bone ... like those of living reptiles, ...en it is likely that they will f ... ogether in the same sort of way. From this starting point we can build up the skeleton, piece by piece, using our knowledge of other animals (and often a lot of common sense) to tell us where each bone should go.

This may take weeks, months or even years of hard work. The pieces

often need to be cleaned of rock and stuck together to make up th skeleton. After this there is still a great deal of work left to do. The next stage is to try to produce a model of the animal as it might have looked when it was alive. From our skeleton we can tell whether the reptile had long legs short, a long neck or a long tail, how big it was and even whether ate meat or plants. We can also tr to rebuild its muscles (see pages 10–11). However, there are a number of things that we cannot do and these should always be remembered when you see models of prehistoric animals – even thos in this book!

First of all, we cannot tell what colour the skin or the eyes of an extinct animal were. Who could have guessed that a zebra had brown and white stripes on its bo

if all there was to go on were its bones! The same applies to small, brightly coloured lizards: we could not possibly know that such animals were so brightly coloured, or that some could even change their colours, if all we had was their skeletons. So, beware, all the pictures of dinosaurs that you see are dressed in purely imaginary colours.

Another problem is that we cannot always tell whether extinct animals had extra soft fleshy parts to their bodies, because again these are not usually preserved in fossils. For example, if elephants were known only as fossils, we could not be sure that they had long flexible trunks or large flapping ears. *Diplodocus*, one of the giant dinosaurs (see pages 40–43), has a rather strange skull: the bony openings for its nostrils were placed not at the end of the snout but on top of the skull between its eyes. This arrangement is found also in elephants and tapirs, both of which have flexible, trunk-like noses. Does this mean that *Diplodocus* had a long, flexible trunk as well?

Above: Supposing all elephants were extinct, a restoration based on the skeleton alone might have produced this trunk-less and almost ear-less animal, since those parts would not have been preserved as fossils.

Left: Found in the Kalahari Desert, this rare lizard belongs to the Family Lacertidae. Most of these lizards are coloured to match their surroundings.

Below: Animals with nostrils near the top of the skull often have long flexible trunks (as do tapirs and elephants). Does this mean that *Diplodocus* too had a trunk?

Messages in stone

All we know about prehistoric animals and, in particular, dinosaurs comes from studying their fossilized remains. What then is a fossil? In its strictest sense a fossil is anything dug out of the ground. Nowadays we use the word to refer to the remains of ancient animals or plants that have been buried in the earth for thousands or millions of years and have turned to stone.

For fossilization (the process by which fossils are formed) to occur, the animal or plant has to be covered quickly by sediment (sand, dust or mud). This stops scavenging animals or the process of decay from destroying its body completely. It is most likely to happen on the sea floor, where small particles of silt and sand, carried down by rivers and currents, are forever settling. Land animals may also become fossilized in this manner if their bodies are washed down-river into a lake or into the sea.

It is usual for only the hard parts of an animal to become fossilized. One way in which the skeleton of an animal can become fossilized is as follows. The soft parts tend to rot and disappear completely. Once buried, the body of a dead animal is gradually covered by more and more layers of sediment. The lower layers become squashed beneath the weight of the upper ones. Very slowly they are compressed into rock. At the same time water, carrying dissolved minerals, seeps through these rocks and through the bones of the buried animal. The minerals tend to be left in the bones, turning them very slowly into stone (that is, they become petrified).

During the many years that it takes for fossils to form, other important natural changes take place. The enormous pressure inside the surface of the Earth makes it heave and buckle. This forms mountains and valleys. In some areas the sea floor is lifted up to form new land, taking the fossils

Above: The feathers and body of *Archaeopteryx* are clearly imprinted on this rock.

Below: Six steps in the process of fossilization. A submerged body is covered in sediments which are then squashed down, forming rock. Percolating minerals turn the bone into stone, and they are exposed by the Earth's movements and subsequent weathering.

  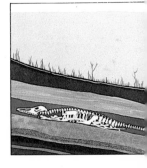

Above: The Grand Canyon, U.S.A., shows how erosion (in this case by the Colorado River cutting into the rock) can reveal the layers of sediment formed over millions of years.

Above: A fossil has to be excavated very carefully. Small knives, dentists' picks and brushes are often the best tools.

Above: Footprint tracks can help palaeontologists understand how extinct animals walked or how fast they ran and even, in some cases, whether or not they lived together in groups.

with it. In this way, fossils originally formed in the sea bed may be found high in the mountains. On land, the layers of sedimentary rock that enclose the fossils are exposed to weathering. These layers are eroded and crumble and crack, so that parts of fossilized animals appear at the surface.

Once a fossil animal has been found, the process of collection begins. First, the site should be marked, photographed and brief notes taken to make a permanent record of its position. Then rock is removed to a level 5–10 centimetres (2–4 inches) above the fossil, using picks, shovels and, sometimes, earthmoving machinery. Next follows the laborious task of carefully removing the rock from around the fossil, using knives, brushes and even small dental tools. The exposed fossil is photographed in detail. Then it is encased in layers of tissue paper and plaster-of-Paris bandages (for protection) and taken back to laboratories for scientific study.

Above and below: The uncovered fossil is photographed and then wrapped in tissues and bandages soaked in plaster of Paris to protect it on its way to the lab.

Fossil jigsaws

It is not very often that a complete fossil skeleton is discovered, with all its bones together in the same position as in life. Usually, before a dead animal on a lake bottom or the sea bed has been completely covered with sediment, its skeleton is disturbed in some way.

Sometimes, as the soft parts which hold the bones together begin to rot, the bones fall away and drift slightly with the water currents so that they end up scattered about. Scavenging animals often help to scatter bones. Occasionally, the bones of a rotting carcass have been scattered by an explosion inside the animal! Bacteria which live in the guts of animals (in human beings too) tend to produce a lot of gas. In a dead animal this can result in the carcass becoming swollen with the pressure of gas until it bursts, releasing the gas and scattering parts of the body across the sea floor.

So we often find a jumble of bones spread over a fairly large area, not necessarily all from the same animal. After all, if two different animals drifted into the same area, their bones might become scattered and therefore mixed together. This gives us a very difficult jigsaw puzzle to solve. We know neither how many pieces there should be in the jigsaw nor whether there is really more than one jigsaw, with several pieces missing from each.

Once a fossil animal is in the laboratory, it is cleaned and studied to find out exactly what the animal might have looked like when it was alive. There are a number of things which can tell us this. If its skeleton is fairly complete, then we may get some idea of how its body was shaped from the way that its bones fit together. A reconstructed skeleton, however, does not really give us an exact picture of how the animal would have looked in life. In many cases it is possible to add the flesh to these skeletons because, where a muscle is attached to a

bone, it often leaves a scar on the surface. Therefore bones are examined for traces of the arrangement of the main muscle groups (particularly those of the jaws, back, shoulders, hips, arms and legs).

Very often we know nothing of the skin of a fossil animal and have to guess what it looked like. However, in some instances, the impression of the skin of an extinct animal is also preserved around its skeleton. Sometimes the mud on which the animal first lay after it died preserved the skin texture (some patches of skin of *Iguanodon* have been found like this).

Sometimes dinosaurs have become mummified and then buried in fine wind-blown sand. This was packed around the tough, sunbaked skin to form a clear mould of its shape (several duck-billed dinosaurs have been found like this). So, from the originally scattered fossil bones, it is often possible to restore the skeleton, flesh it out and, in some cases, even show what its skin was like.

However, it is also very easy to make serious mistakes when trying

to draw a picture of a complete animal based on a few of its bone This happened when models were first made of *Iguanodon*. The tee which had been found, like those a modern iguana but very much bigger, were thought to have belonged to a giant extinct lizard; their owner was therefore called *Iguanodon*, which means 'iguana tooth' in ancient Greek (scholars tended to give their finds Latin or

Right: After the skeleton of a dinosaur, in this case *Iguanodon*, has been reconstructed, the next stage is restoration of its muscles, using as clues the muscle scars on its bones to give an idea of the general shape and proportions of the animal. Finally, a textured substance resembling the animal's skin is added to the restoration.

skeleton

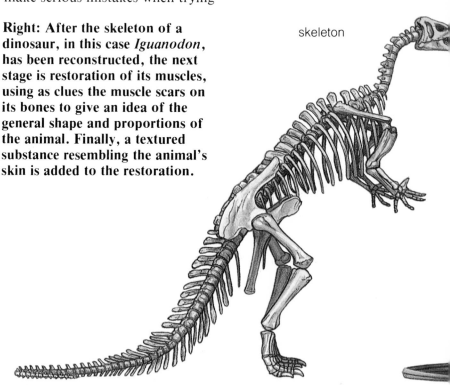

reek names so that they might be
sily understood throughout the
ucated world). Some time later a
w leg bones and some back bones
longing to the same animal were
und. From a study of these finds,
model was built that looked rather
e a reptilian rhinoceros; it was
en given a large conical bone
its nose, like a horn. This
inoceros-like restoration of
uanodon was used for many years
til, in 1878, several complete
uanodon skeletons were found
Belgium. These showed that
e animal stood upright on its
ck legs and that the 'nose
rn' was really the end of its
ky thumb.

**ft: Some *Iguanodon* teeth
covered in the Wealden area of
uth-East England.**

**ght: This restoration of
uanodon was completed in 1854
r the Great Exhibition when it
s moved from Hyde Park to
ystal Palace in South London.**

skeleton
and muscle

complete
reconstruction

11

BEFORE DINOSAURS
Ages of Earth

1st January

The beginning of the earth
4500 million years ago

Ever since the Earth was formed (about 4500 million years ago) the weathering process has been wearing down its crust. The products of this erosion are washed down into the valleys, the lakes and, in particular, the sea. There they form layer upon layer of sediments containing the remains of dead animals and plants. These layers (strata) become compressed by the weight above to form rocks; the rocks may eventually be heaved up out of the sea by movements of the Earth's crust to form mountains, and then the whole process can begin all over again. The history of the Earth and of the animals and plants that lived long ago is therefore locked away in rocks all over the world. Unfortunately there is no single complete set of rocks representing the whole of the time that has passed from the Earth's formation to the present. However, there are sequences of rocks scattered around the globe which, together, represent most of the Earth's history.

Over long periods of time animal and plant species change their structure and appearance (or *evolve*), so fossils are very useful for comparing the ages of the different rocks in which they are found. For instance, if rocks from different areas contain the same types of fossil, then we can be fairly sure that the rocks are of about the same age.

Life on Earth began more than 3000 million years ago with very simple bacteria-like organisms. Their fossilized remains have been found in rocks in Zimbabwe in southern Africa. To give some idea of how long ago that was, compared with when dinosaurs lived or when Man first appeared, we have used a diagram (see right) to condense the 4500 million years since the Earth was formed into a single year of 365 days.

1st September

Quaternary

Cainozoic Era

Tertiary — early horse — modern frog — flowers — million years ago

Mesozoic Era

Cretaceous

The Age of the Dinosaurs

Jurassic — Boxing Day

Triassic — 14th December

Permian — Youngina — sail-backs — 28

Carboniferous — dragonfly — shark

Devonian — Dinichthys — amphibian

Silurian — crinoid — plants — eurypterid

Ordovician — cup coral — brachiopod — crinoid

Cambrian — brachiopod — echinoderm — trilobite

Precambrian

Palaeozoic Era

1st February

1st October

19th October green algae appear

1st March

1st November

first life forms appear (bacteria) 26th March

an appears at 5 p.m.
n New Year's Eve

he mammals take over
om the dinosaurs

Earth's history compressed into a single year. Note that about 4000 million years were taken up by the Precambrian. Some of

the groups from the Mesozoic Era, Age of Dinosaurs, are illustrated in the expanded sections.

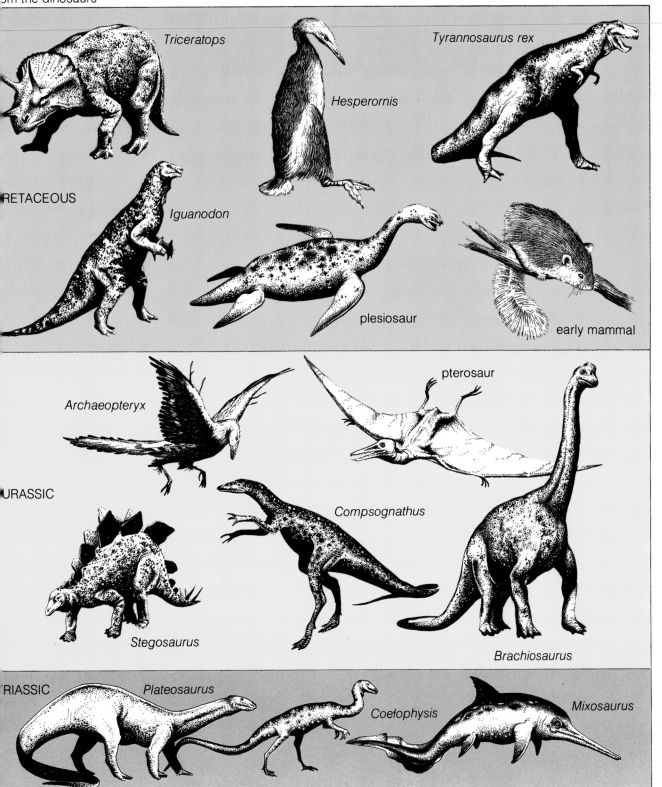

Triceratops

Hesperornis

Tyrannosaurus rex

RETACEOUS

Iguanodon

plesiosaur

early mammal

pterosaur

Archaeopteryx

URASSIC

Compsognathus

Stegosaurus

Brachiosaurus

RIASSIC   Plateosaurus

Coelophysis

Mixosaurus

Life in the ancient seas

Before we look at the details of the real stars of this book, the dinosaurs, perhaps we should first consider the animals that lived earlier. After all, although the first dinosaurs appeared as long ago as 200 million years, many interesting and unusual animals had lived on Earth for hundreds of millions of years before this. By looking at these earlier creatures we can get some idea of the way that life has evolved on our planet, how the dinosaurs came to be and where they fit into the history of life on Earth.

Our story goes back to the Palaeozoic Era. From before this Era (in Precambrian time) only a few very simple fossils are known.

Right: Trilobites made up 60 per cent of all known creatures at the beginning of the Palaeozoic Era. Although they had died out by the end of the Palaeozoic, they had once been its most advanced animals.

Cambrian Period

Ordovician Period

wever, at the beginning of the mbrian Period (the first period of Palaeozoic Era) a large variety complex sea animals suddenly peared. Was there really a sudden h of animal life, and, if so, y? Nobody knows the answers these questions, but one portant change did take place at t time. Several groups of animals eloped the ability to make mselves hard, limy shells, which ld more easily be preserved as sils. We can therefore find well-served fossils of trilobites, chiopods, eocrinoids and many er Cambrian animals.

The trilobites were common mals in these ancient seas. They t appeared in the Cambrian but, er the following Ordovician riod, they seem to have dwindled number and variety. Finally, at end of the Palaeozoic Era, they appeared altogether.

There appeared in the oceans of Ordovician a group of predatory animals called eurypterids (or 'sea scorpions'). They looked a little like real scorpions, with a pair of ferocious-looking pincers, four pairs of walking legs and, at the rear, a pair of paddles to help them swim. The early forms were quite small, about 10 centimetres (4 inches) long, but some truly enormous eurypterids appeared during the Silurian Period. Again, like the trilobites, the eurypterids dwindled and disappeared before the end of the Palaeozoic Era.

The fossilized remains of a few fishes have been found in Ordovician and Silurian rocks, but it was not until the Devonian Period that fishes became common. Many of the earliest fishes were heavily armoured with bony plates, probably for protection against the large eurypterids which undoubtedly preyed upon them. These first fishes, called ostracoderms (or bony-skins), were quite small, less than 40 centimetres (16 inches) long. They had no jaws and their mouths were holes or slits through which they sucked food.

1 *Marrella* (primitive arthropod)
2 Jellyfish
3 Echinoderms
4 Various sponges
5 *Ellipsocephalus* (a trilobite)
6 *Paradoxides* (a trilobite)
7 Nautiloids (straight, coiled)
8 *Cryptolithus* (a trilobite)
9 Cup corals
10 Early sea urchins

11 Brachiopods (lamp shells)
12 Early snail
13 *Pterygotus* (a sea scorpion)
14 Coral colonies
15 *Tryplasma* (horn coral)
16 Nautiloid (coiled)
17 *Cladoselache* (early shark)
18 Spiny trilobite
19 *Hemicyclaspis* (jawless fish)
20 *Pteraspis* (jawless fish)

Silurian Period

Devonian Period

From water to land

The Devonian Period is often called the Age of Fishes, because of the large number and variety of fishes that developed at that time. Many jawless ostracoderms survived, but, more important, the first fishes with jaws evolved. These new fishes became extremely successful, because, with sharp teeth lining their jaws, they were able to feed on all kinds of plants and animals. The ancestors of all the fishes of today were among these early jawed fishes.

One group of fishes very numerous in the Devonian were the 'lobe-fins', so called because each fin had a muscular base containing a series of bones. These fishes are particularly interesting, because it is within this group that a most

important evolutionary change took place. At some stage in the Late Devonian a lobe-finned fish succeeded in leaving the water to start a new life on the land as an amphibian. Three questions immediately crop up when we consider this remarkable change. Which fish was it that managed to crawl on to the land? How was this change brought about? (After all, most fishes that are taken out of water die very quickly.) And why did it need to live on the land at all?

As yet we do not know exactly which fish was the first to walk on land. However, some fossil fishes are known which must have been very closely related to this creature. To survive on land an animal must

be able to breathe air and move about without difficulty. Lobe-finned fishes already possessed these two essential adaptations for land life.

One 'lobe-fin' named *Eusthenopteron* has been studied i minute detail for evidence of its land-living abilities. Some of its fi bones have been found to be simil to those in the legs of the first amphibians. From a study of the way in which these fin bones might have moved, it seems likely that *Eusthenopteron* could have used its fins as simple legs or prop to crawl on land.

It must also have had a lung for breathing air; for, although no actual lung has been found in the fossils, lungs are still present in

ving relatives of these early lobe-
ns, the 'lung fishes' of South
merica, Africa and Australia.
/ith these two features, a lobe-
nned fish would have been able to
urvive on land for at least a short
eriod. To stay longer on land the
obe-fin' would need to evolve
elids to prevent its eyes from
rying out, a thick skin to stop the
ody drying too quickly and ears to
ear air-borne noises.

Finally, why did fishes want to
ove on to land at all? One theory
uggests that limbs might have
olved in fishes which fed on
sects and grubs along the edges of
reams. If these fishes were small
id light enough, they could have
ed their fins to haul themselves
it on to the muddy banks. The

fins would have gradually evolved
into legs, making these fishes the
first land-living amphibians.

One of the earliest fossil
amphibians that we know is
Ichthyostega, which grew to about
1 metre (3 feet) long. It was found
in Greenland in rocks of the latest
Devonian and had short, powerful
legs, a large flat head, scaly skin and
a long tail with a fish-like tail fin.

Although *Ichthyostega* was one
of the earliest amphibians, it was
certainly not the very first.
Remains of two more amphibians
have been found in Greenland and
North America and, since they
lived at the same time as
Ichthyostega, it is likely that their
common ancestor must have
appeared even earlier.

**Below: The scene below shows
some of the typical inhabitants of
a Devonian coal swamp. To the
left can be seen the predatory
lobe-finned fish *Eusthenopteron*.
On its underside are pairs of lobed
fins with the thick muscular bases.
In the foreground two young
Eusthenopteron have hauled
themselves out on to the bank,
using their strong lobed fins like
legs. The large animal on the right is
the early amphibian, *Ichthyostega*.
It looks like a larger version of
Eusthenopteron – it even has a fish-
like tail – but it has short, powerful
walking legs. The back of another
Ichthyostega is just visible above
the surface of the water in the
background. They probably preyed
upon fish such as *Eusthenopteron*.**

First reptiles

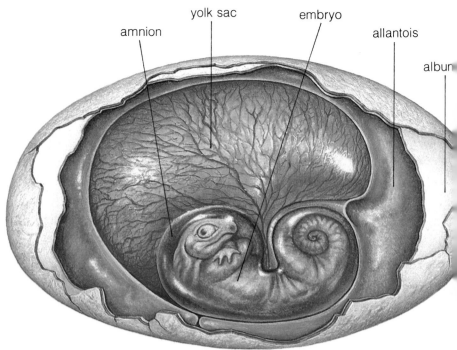

amnion　yolk sac　embryo　allantois

albun

It was during the Carboniferous Period that reptiles evolved from amphibians. Amphibians, unlike reptiles, never became completely independent of the water. The critical difference between a reptile and an amphibian was that the reptile had evolved an amniotic egg (surrounded by membranes and enclosed within a shell). Such an egg could safely be laid even in the dry areas on land without drying out.

The earliest fossil reptile is *Hylonomus*, which was found in Nova Scotia, Canada. It lived in mid-Carboniferous times and was a small animal, about 20 centimetres (8 inches) long; it probably fed on insect-like animals. This lizard-like creature seems to have been quite successful and evolved into a range of larger reptiles in the later Carboniferous and Permian times.

One particular group of reptiles, called the synapsids, separated off at the very beginning. These were the first in a long line of animals which eventually evolved into mammals, some of which, in turn, evolved into the human species.

The earlier synapsids, called pelycosaurs, were quite large

animals; most of them were predators, catching amphibians and fish. Later, in the early part of the Permian Period, pelycosaurs like *Dimetrodon* evolved a row of tall bony spines which probably supported a thin 'sail' along the middle of the back. These 'sail-back' synapsids had a big advantage over other reptiles living at the time. Modern reptiles are typically 'cold-blooded', which means that, on a cold day, they remain cold and can move only very slowly, but on a hot sunny day they become warm and active.

Above: A typical reptile egg, showing the developing embryoni reptile, the yolk sac (its food stor the allantois (its waste container a air-breathing sac), the amnion (fil with cushioning fluid) and the albumen (a water and food reserve).

Below, left to right: The pelycosaurs *Dimetrodon*, in the background, and *Ophiacodon*, in the foreground; the early therapsi *Lycaenops*; the later therapsid *Thrinaxodon*; and the early true mammal *Megazostrodon*.

Dimetrodon

Ophiacodon

Above: *Hylonomus* was a small, lizard-like animal. Its remains have been found preserved in Carboniferous tree stumps in Nova Scotia. *Hylonomus* almost certainly laid an egg with a shell, like the one shown above.

Sail-backs like *Dimetrodon* could use their sails to obtain warmth from the sun. They therefore may have become active before the other, sail-less reptiles and could simply walk about and eat their still-cold, sluggish relatives! Despite the advantages of a sail, these sail-backs died out later in the Permian. They were replaced by another group of synapsids called the therapsids.

The therapsids, which first appeared in the Middle Permian, gradually became more and more like mammals until, just before the end of the Triassic Period, the first true mammal, the tiny *Megazostrodon*, appeared. Modern mammals differ from modern reptiles in several ways. They are 'warm-blooded' and their skin is covered with fur to keep in the heat; they give birth to live young; they have many different types of teeth for breaking up food; and their legs are tucked underneath their bodies so that they can run faster. *Lycaenops* from the Permian and *Thrinaxodon* from the early Triassic show some of these mammal characters evolving. *Lycaenops* had quite long legs, partly erect; it had teeth of different sizes and shapes; and it may have been at least partly 'warm-blooded'. But, like a reptile, it still had scaly skin and laid eggs. The smaller *Thrinaxodon* had similar erect legs and had very complicated chewing teeth. Like reptiles, it probably still laid eggs.

Megazostrodon was a true mammal because it gave birth to live young. All the early mammals seem to have been tiny animals which fed on insects after dark. They could not come out by day because dinosaurs had evolved by this time (the late Triassic) and may have eaten them.

Lycaenops

Thrinaxodon

Megazostrodon

The reptile family tree

Right: This chart traces the history of some of the reptile groups during the Mesozoic Era, when reptiles ruled the land.

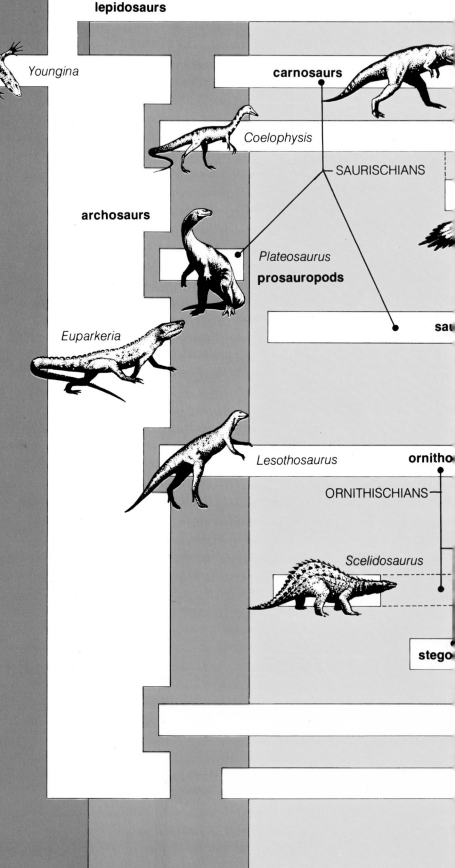

lepidosaurs

diapsids   *Youngina*

carnosaurs

Coelophysis

— SAURISCHIANS

archosaurs

Plateosaurus

prosauropods

sau

Euparkeria

Lesothosaurus

ornitho

ORNITHISCHIANS —

Scelidosaurus

stego

The earliest reptiles, like *Hylonomus*, seem to have evolved from smaller ancestors of amphibians like *Ichthyostega* in the early part of the Carboniferous Period. So far as we can tell, little reptiles like *Hylonomus* were the ancestors of all the later reptiles, birds and mammals (including ourselves). Four main groups of reptile evolved from these tiny early reptiles. The only present-day survivors of the most primitive group (called anapsids) are the turtles and tortoises. Another group (called the euryapsids) is completely extinct; it included the aquatic placodonts, plesiosaurs and ichthyosaurs. The other two groups, and their descendants, have dominated the land for the last 250 million years.

One of these successful groups was the synapsids, which were the dominant land vertebrates until the reign of the dinosaurs began. After the dinosaurs died out 65 million years ago the synapsids' descendants, the mammals, staged a come-back and have remained dominant ever since. The other great group, the diapsids, was split into two types: the lepidosaurs (lizards and snakes) and the archosaurs (crocodiles, dinosaurs, pterodactyls and their relatives). The lizards and snakes have changed comparatively little in their history, and so we turn to the dinosaurs. The first archosaurs appeared at the end of the Permian. The first dinosaurs evolved toward the end of the Triassic Period and persisted for 140 million years before going extinct at the end of the Cretaceous Period.

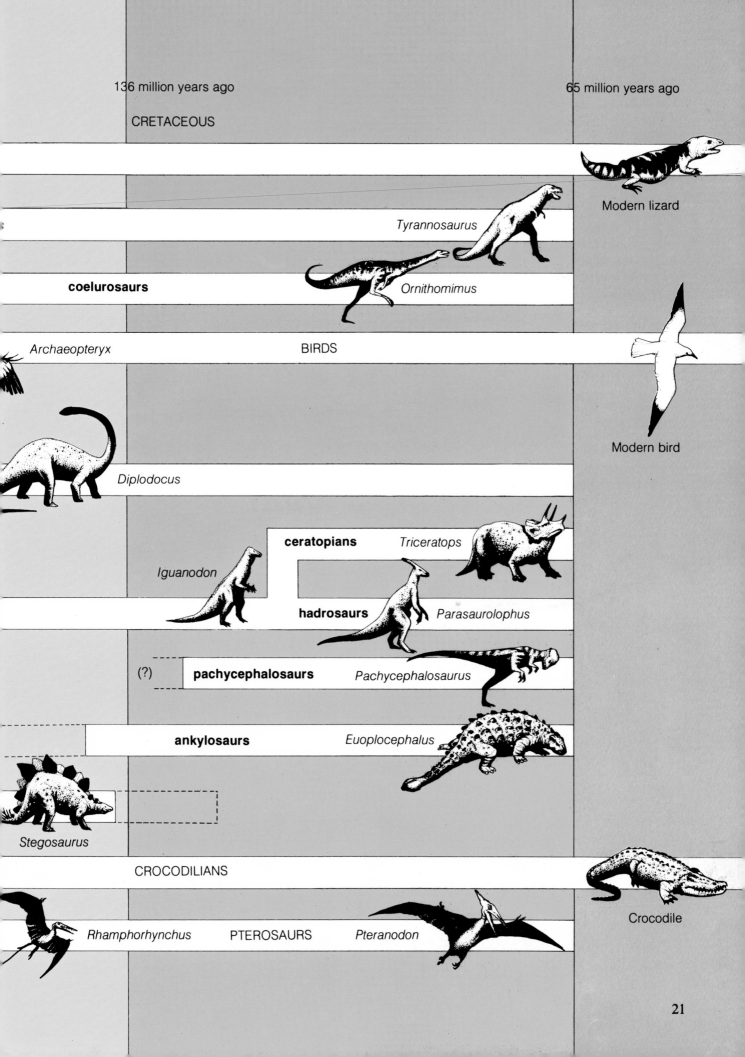

136 million years ago

65 million years ago

CRETACEOUS

Modern lizard

Tyrannosaurus

coelurosaurs

Ornithomimus

Archaeopteryx

BIRDS

Modern bird

Diplodocus

ceratopians

Triceratops

Iguanodon

hadrosaurs

Parasaurolophus

(?)

pachycephalosaurs

Pachycephalosaurus

ankylosaurs

Euoplocephalus

Stegosaurus

CROCODILIANS

Crocodile

Rhamphorhynchus   PTEROSAURS   *Pteranodon*

21

Origin of the dinosaurs

The dinosaurs are grouped with a variety of other reptiles such as pterodactyls and crocodiles which, all together, are called archosaurs (meaning 'ruling reptiles'). These creatures all share a characteristic arrangement of holes in their skulls. Their particular pattern of holes is different from that in other reptiles and means that a very complicated arrangement of powerful muscles can be attached around the edges of these holes and on to the lower jaw, giving these animals a very strong bite. Another possible reason for these holes is that they provided space for the creature's jaw muscles to bulge into.

Dinosaurs are classed as a separate group within the main group of archosaurs because, like the mammals (see pages 18–19), they managed to bring their legs completely underneath their bodies, rather than having them sticking out sideways as do other reptiles such as lizards. As a result, the

dinosaurs were able to take much longer strides and run very much faster than other reptiles; this proved to be a great advantage both for catching prey and escaping from predators.

But from where did the archosaurs come? And when did the first dinosaurs evolve? These questions are not easy to answer because we do not have a complete fossil record of these animals at the time when they were first evolving.

To discover from which group of reptiles the archosaurs evolved, we have first to look for the oldest fossil reptiles that have the archosaurian pattern of holes in the skull. Then we have to find even older fossil reptiles that have started to develop some, but not all, of these holes.

Such a reptile lived during the Permian Period, a small lizard-like creature called *Youngina*. It is important because the sides of its

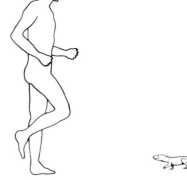

Above: *Euparkeria*'s size compar with modern man's. Man is abou 1.8 metres (6 feet); *Euparkeria* was only 60 centimetres (2 feet) long.

Below: Fossil remains of *Euparke* have been found in parts of Sout Africa.

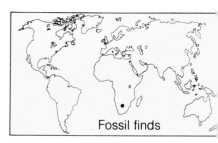

Fossil finds

ull had some, but not all, of the ...les that are found in archosaurs. ...erefore, until a more likely fossil ...d is made, *Youngina* seems ...ossible ancestor of the ...chosaurs which, after 25 million ...rs, might have evolved the extra ...les in their skulls and grown ...ch larger.

The oldest true archosaurs, the ...oterosuchians, lived at about ... end of the Permian and the ...ginning of the Triassic. They ...oked a little like modern ...ocodiles.

The fossil remains of an ...eresting little archosaur named ...parkeria* have been found in ...uth Africa in rocks which date

back to the early part of the Triassic Period. It had a double row of bony armour down its back, a long tail and long, powerful back legs. *Euparkeria* grew to about 1 metre (3 feet) long and probably lived on lizards and large insects. It may be that, although it spent most of its time running on all fours, it could make a quick dash – rearing up on its back legs with its tail stuck out as a balancer. This ability would have been extremely useful to *Euparkeria* because it lived at the same time as some of the large flesh-eating therapsids and it could have made a rapid escape if attacked by these fierce animals. It would also have meant that *Euparkeria* could have

made surprise attacks on its own prey.

From what we know of little *Euparkeria* it seems to show the beginnings of features seen in the dinosaurs later in the Triassic Period.

Below: Two *Euparkeria* scamper about in search of a meal of locusts. The large, threatening figure of the meat-eating therapsid, *Cynognathus* (see pages 18–19), would not have concerned *Euparkeria* because they could probably easily out-run the larger, clumsy therapsid.

The time of change

It would be wonderful to travel back to the Triassic Period so that we need not rely on fossils alone for our knowledge. This was a very crucial time in the history of life on Earth; it was then that two great groups of animals, the therapsids (the ancestors of the mammals, see pages 18–19), and the early archosaurs (the ancestors of the dinosaurs and birds) were both evolving rapidly in the race to become the most successful of the large land animals. Both groups of reptile are found together right up until the end of the Triassic Period. Then, quite suddenly, the archosaurs, or rather the *dinosaurs*, are found alone.

In the Early Triassic the therapsids were the most numerous group of large land animals. There were great herds of pig-like plant-eating therapsids called dicynodonts and many sharp-toothed, predatory cynodonts (some of which might have grown as large as the lions of Africa today!). On the other hand the archosaurs were, on the whole, rather small, fleet-footed animals like *Euparkeria* (see pages 22–3).

By middle Triassic times, about 10 to 15 million years later (that is, about 210 million years ago), the scene had not really changed a great deal, in that similar sorts of animal were clearly still in existence. However, the relative numbers of the animals present had changed, indicating the degree of success of each group. The herds of dicynodonts had dwindled, and the flesh-eating cynodonts were not only less numerous, but were also smaller in size (about the size of a fox rather than that of a lion). A new group of reptiles, named rhynchosaurs, also appeared (see *Stenaulorhynchus* below). These

rhynchosaurs were rather pig-like appearance (somewhat similar to t dicynodonts, which they seem to have partly replaced) with a tubby body, short legs and most peculia jaws. The upper jaw had, at the front, a sharp, chisel-like beak, rather like a parrot's, and it could be chopped down against a groove in the lower jaw. Hundreds of sm teeth on the jaws behind the beak formed very rough surfaces, rathe like files, for grinding food. The powerful beak and grinding teeth were probably used for feeding on tough roots and stems which the

Above: The large Middle Triassic archosaur, *Mandasuchus*, wanders off after feeding on the plump, short-legged rhynchosaur, *Stenaulorhynchus*. **Notice the semi-erect position of *Mandasuchus*'s legs, holding its belly clear of the ground.**

t: *Mandasuchus* (also see below)
w to about 2.5 metres (8 feet)
g.

ht: Fossil remains of this type of
mal have been found at sites as
wn on the map.

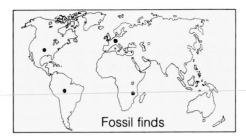

Fossil finds

nchosaurs dug out of the
und. Alongside these animals
d larger archosaurs such as
ndasuchus (see below). These
e descendants of *Euparkeria*-like
mals and still had the long
werful tail and rows of bony
nour down the back. They grew
3–4 metres (10–13 feet) in length
l were all flesh-eaters. Although
have not yet found many
ndasuchus fossils, we can guess
t they were quite successful; they
e the largest animals of their
e and were able to draw their
s beneath their bodies.

With this improved ability to
move, these Middle Triassic
archosaurs were well able to chase
and capture their prey, the plant-
eating therapsids and rhynchosaurs.
This probably made life very
competitive for the other flesh-
eating group, the cynodonts, which
were quite quick-moving predators
like the archosaurs. They perhaps
tended to chase alternative sources
of food, such as small lizards and
insects, rather than competing with
the archosaurs. Thus, by the end of
Middle Triassic times, the two main
groups had seemingly changed

places: the archosaurs, which had
started out in the Early Triassic
as small insect- and lizard-eaters,
had become large meat-eaters,
while the therapsids, which
started out as large meat-
eaters, ended up as insect- and
lizard-eaters!

By Late Triassic times the
rhynchosaurs had practically
disappeared; the few remaining
therapsids and the newly evolved
mammals (see pages 18–19) were
mostly reduced to tiny nocturnal
animals.

The archosaurs, however, had
become very abundant and
included not only some forms
which still looked rather like
Mandasuchus but the very first
dinosaurs: archosaurs which had
brought their legs under their bodies
completely (like dogs or horses) and
could presumably run very fast
indeed.

Origin of the plant-eaters

The earliest fossilized remains of true dinosaurs appear in rocks laid down at the end of the Triassic. They presumably evolved from some of the earlier Middle Triassic archosaurs, of which *Mandasuchus* (see pages 24–25) is an example. These early dinosaurs were not the spectacular giants that we think of whenever the name dinosaur is mentioned, but some were nevertheless extremely large and fearsome creatures.

The name 'dinosaur' in fact refers to two very distinct groups of reptile, the **saurischian** (or lizard-hipped) dinosaurs and the **ornithischian** (or bird-hipped) forms. These two groups are distinguished by the way their hip bones are arranged and the structure of their lower jaws (see page 32).

There were two very different types of early saurischian dinosaurs: the medium to large **prosauropods** such as *Massospondylus* and *Plateosaurus*, which may have eaten both animal and vegetable food (see pages 28–9), and the smaller, nimble **coelurosaurs** such as *Coelophysis* (see pages 30–31). The

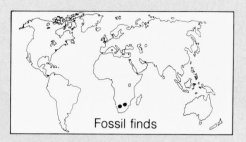

Above right: *Massospondylus* grew to a length of between 4–6 metres (13–20 feet).

Above: Fossil remains have been found in southern Africa.

early ornithischian dinosaurs were all rather small, **ornithopods**, fleet-footed plant-eaters such as *Lesothosaurus* (see pages 32–3).

In the early part of the late Triassic, the saurischian dinosaurs such as *Massospondylus* were faced with an interesting biological problem. As we have seen (pages 24–5) the Middle Triassic archosaurs preyed on the plant-eating reptiles of the time, the rhynchosaurs, cynodonts and dicynodonts. They did this so thoroughly that by the end of the

Below: In this scene two *Massospondylus* **can be seen feeding. Although we are fairly s**▪ **that** *Massospondylus* **ate plants much of the time, it is possible th**▪ **it also ate insects.**

Middle Triassic these plant-eaters had almost disappeared and the archosaurs were left with very littl▪ on which to feed. There was less meat; but, with the plant-eating therapsids nearly extinct, there was much more vegetable food available. The obvious answer to the problem (if this interpretation▪ correct) was that some of the earl▪ dinosaurs should become plant-eaters, and some of them did just that. From the evidence available it seems that *Massospondylus* probably had a mixed diet of mea▪

plants, although its ancestors
e probably very like
ndasuchus and were meat-eaters
of the time. We have come to
conclusion because we know
t the teeth of *Mandasuchus* were
rp and pointed, and had tiny
rations running down their edges,
like steak knives. Therefore,
y were ideal for cutting meat but
less for chewing plants. If we
k at the teeth of an animal such
Massospondylus, however, we
l that they were smaller and less
nted, and perhaps better adapted
mixed diet. *Massospondylus*
had a large bulky body and a
ll head, which is further
dence that it was more like a
nt-eater than a meat-eater. Meat-

eaters usually have larger heads with
long stabbing teeth and slimmer
bodies adapted for fast running to
catch their prey.

The large size of *Massospondylus*
(5 metres [16 feet] or more long)
would have discouraged all but the
most ferocious of predators. But, if
attacked, it had a remarkable
defensive weapon. Its hands had
unusually long thumb claws which
were curved and sharp. When
threatened, *Massospondylus* would
probably rear up on its back legs
and slash at the face and eyes of its
attacker.

Safety in numbers

One of the best known of the early **prosauropod** saurischian dinosaurs is *Plateosaurus*. The remains of many skeletons of this dinosaur were found in a quarry in Trossingen, southern Germany, early in this century. *Plateosaurus* was rather similar to *Massospondylus* (see pages 26–7) in shape, although it was rather larger, up to 6–7 metres (20–23 feet) in length.

The discovery of a large number of skeletons of one particular type of animal is always of great interest to palaeontologists (people who study fossils). Such a find raises the question: how did so many animals come to be together at the moment of death? Was it purely by accident, or does it show that they moved around in family groups and herds? In the case of *Plateosaurus* it looks very much as though they were animals that lived together in herds. Some of their remains have been preserved and show that groups of them moving about together have been caught in a flash flood. This suggests that the animals probably found safety in numbers. Although the flesh-eating dinosaurs were slightly smaller than *Plateosaurus*, a lone *Plateosaurus* would not have been able to defend itself very well and would eventually have lost to a determined attacker. However, grouped together, the plateosaurs stood a far better chance of fighting off a flesh-eater. As part of a herd, they were also in a better position to protect their young ones; when moving from place to place to find fresh food, they would probably have kept in strict formation, with the young ones and females at the centre of the herd and the larger, stronger males around the outside.

Plateosaurus probably ate nothing but plants. Its teeth were quite small and leaf-shaped as you would expect in an animal that did not need strong, sharp teeth to rip at tough hide and raw flesh. However, none of *Plateosaurus*'s teeth seems to have been worn flat, as is usually the case when the teeth are used to chop up plant food. This unusual condition suggests that *Plateosaurus* used its teeth rather like a rake to strip leaves and shoots from the trees. The food would then be swallowed whole, without being chewed, and ground into fragments by pieces of stone kept inside their stomachs. This might seem an odd thing to do, but crocodiles today (distant relations of these dinosaurs) are known to swallow stones, which they keep in their stomachs and use as ballast and for grinding up food. Moreover, some early dinosaur skeletons have been discovered with piles of small stones within their bodies, just where you would expect the stomach to have been.

Plant food, weight for weight, is much less nutritious than meat, therefore animals that eat plants tend to have rather large stomachs to hold the larger quantities of plant food they need to provide them with enough energy. Plant food also takes a long time to be digested, or broken down into a form that the animals can use, so their stomachs have to be big enough to store the food while they wait for this to happen.

This fact has led us to the realization of one of the less obvious advantages of developing legs that are held erect beneath the body. With legs in this position, like pillars, the weight of the body can be carried more efficiently than it can with legs akimbo as in the more primitive reptiles. Therefore the pillar-like legs of the dinosaurs enabled them to grow much larger, especially the plant-eaters, whose legs had to support a large body. *Plateosaurus* was one of the largest land animals of the Late Triassic. Indeed this group of plant-eaters is related to the largest land animals that ever lived, the **sauropod** dinosaurs of the Jurassic and Cretaceous Periods (see pages 40–43).

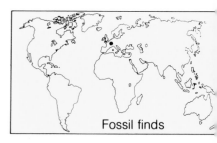

Fossil finds

low: A large herd of
teosaurus has broken
mation. The noise of a violent
rm has sent many of the
unger animals running in fright
d they are now being hastily
inded up by their anxious
ents. Meanwhile the larger

males are scouting the area for
predators.

Left: Fossils of *Plateosaurus* were
found in southern Germany.

Right: *Plateosaurus* was 6 metres (20
feet) long and 3 metres (10 feet) high,

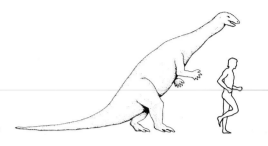

The first nimble hunter

The saurischian dinosaurs of the Late Triassic include not only the large **prosauropod** plant-eaters but also another group of very different-looking saurischians called **coelurosaurs**. *Coelophysis* (see below), which has been found in large numbers in Triassic rocks in New Mexico, U.S.A., is a fairly typical member of this group. Unlike prosauropods (see pages 26–7 and 28–9), they ate only meat and were also noticeably smaller. *Coelophysis* grew to a maximum length of about 2.5 metres (8 feet).

It was because they needed to hunt the animals on which they fed, because their food was less bulky (thus requiring a smaller stomach), that the coelurosaurs were smaller and more lightly built than the plant-eaters. Indeed, they were rather nimble-looking animals. The small body of these reptiles was easily balanced by the long tail, enabling them to stand, walk or run on their two back legs alone. (The front legs were never needed as legs and could therefore be used as arms.) Some of the early plant-eaters such as *Plateosaurus* (see pages 28–9) could also balance on their back legs, although most of their time was spent on all fours. The back legs of coelurosaurs became longer and stronger for running fast and the feet became extraordinarily bird-like, with thr long, foward-pointing toes and tl smaller, inner toe pointing backwards behind the foot. In *Coelophysis* the arms were much shorter than the legs and the han had three long, clawed fingers which could be used for catching prey. The neck was long and slender, presumably so that it cou be arched downwards and allow head to bite at prey held in its she arms. The slender, pointed head was small in proportion to the re of the body; the teeth were small but sharp and curved backwards as to grip the prey firmly. It seem

ikely that an animal the size of *elophysis*, no matter how ~~o~~cious, would have been able to ~~a~~ck the much larger plant-eaters ~~h~~ as *Plateosaurus*. Most ~~pr~~obably it fed on smaller animals ~~suc~~h as insects, lizards and even ~~sm~~all amphibians such as frogs and ~~toa~~ds (see below) when it could find ~~the~~m. A few of the many fossilized ~~ske~~letons of *Coelophysis* found in ~~Ne~~w Mexico, on closer examination, ~~we~~re seen to contain parts of very ~~sm~~all *Coelophysis* skeletons. It ~~loo~~ks suspiciously as though some ~~Co~~*elophysis* were behaving like ~~can~~nibals and eating their young; ~~eith~~er that, or *Coelophysis* gave

birth to live young. None of these coelurosaurs grew large enough to threaten the plant-eaters, but this does not mean that they were not successful; many different types of coelurosaur survived right to the end of the dinosaurs' reign, as will be seen later.

There was also another group of large early archosaurs, not proper dinosaurs, that survived into the Late Triassic. One was called *Ornithosuchus* and its bones have been discovered in Scotland. It grew to about 4 metres (13 feet) long, had long back legs, quite short front legs and a very large head, the jaws of which were lined with long stabbing teeth. It seems to have been a ferocious animal and may well have attacked the large early plant-eaters. We do not call *Ornithosuchus* a true dinosaur because it still had armour, a double row of bony plates down its back, and it had not succeeded in bringing its legs right under its body in the same way as true dinosaurs, more like *Euparkeria* (see pages 22–3) and *Mandasuchus* (see pages 24–5) of the earlier parts of the Triassic.

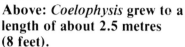

Above: *Coelophysis* grew to a length of about 2.5 metres (8 feet).

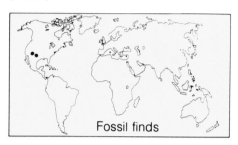

Fossil finds

Above: Bones of *Coelophysis* have been found in Late Triassic rocks in Arizona and New Mexico.

Below: A tiny movement made by a small, colourful Triassic frog, disturbed by a passing *Coelophysis*, has revealed its position. With a quick change of direction, *Coelophysis* gives chase and is ready to catch this tasty morsel in its sharply clawed hands.

Hips like a bird's

We have already seen three of the earliest types of saurischian dinosaur: two fairly large prosauropods and a nimble little coelurosaur. Now we come to the other great group mentioned earlier: the ornithischian dinosaurs (see Glossary).

The earliest ornithischian dinosaur known is a small **ornithopod** named *Pisanosaurus*, the partial remains of which have been found in rocks of Upper Triassic age in Argentina. The shape of its teeth suggests that it was a plant-eating animal; it had long back legs and, most important of all, its hip bones may have been arranged in a way that is peculiar to the ornithischian type of dinosaur. This arrangement resembles that in the hips of birds; indeed the name 'ornithischian' means 'bird-hipped' However, birds and ornithischian dinosaurs are not closely related. It seems very likely that *Pisanosaurus* looked much like another, better-known ornithischian dinosaur named *Lesothosaurus*, which has been found in Upper Triassic rocks in southern Africa.

Lesothosaurus was a small ornithopod (not more than 1 metre [3 feet] long) resembling *Coelophysis* (see pages 30–31) in its general appearance. It had a slim body, balanced at the hips by a long tail, and long spindly legs for fast running; the short arms were equipped with five fingers and short, blunt claws, used for grasping the leaves and shoots upon which the animal fed. (All ornithischian dinosaurs were plant-eaters.) The head of *Lesothosaurus* was fairly small, with small leaf-shaped teeth lining the jaws. These teeth were used for slicing shoots and stems. Another feature found only among the ornithischian dinosaurs was a toothless bone in the middle of the front of the lower jaw (probably covered during life by a layer of horn). In *Lesothosaurus* this *predentary* bone was extremely small and restricted to the very tip of the lower jaw, unlike the turtle-like beak of the larger ornithischian dinosaur

Camptosaurus (see pages 44–5). Since the predentary is a feature of all ornithischian dinosaurs, it should be possible to tell at a glance which dinosaurs in this book are ornithischians.

Lesothosaurus seems to have been one of the most primitive of all ornithischian dinosaurs, because it appears not to have had cheeks. All other ornithischians show some evidence of muscular cheeks covering the sides of their mouths – mainly to prevent plant food from spilling out of the sides of their mouth while chewing.

Lesothosaurus was small enough to be preyed upon by the fleet-footed coelurosaurs of the time. So agility, small size and high speed

Above: A male and female *Lesothosaurus* mating. Mating a reproduction in dinosaurs is poor understood. Nor is it known how enormous dinosaurs like *Brachiosaurus* managed to lay eggs without breaking them.

Below: *Lesothosaurus* bones have been found in late Triassic rocks Lesotho, southern Africa.

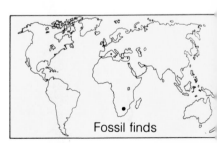

Fossil finds

re essential to avoid such
dators; after all, *Lesothosaurus*
l no weapons either for defence
for retaliation.

Living at about the same time as
sothosaurus*, and also in southern
rica, was another small
nithischian dinosaur named
terodontosaurus*. It was rather
ilar in appearance to
sothosaurus* and was obviously
ther fast-running plant-eater.
wever, it did have one rather
narkable difference: near the
nt of both its upper and lower
rs was a pair of small tusks,
ighter versions of those found in
jaws of present-day wild pigs.
terodontosaurus* may have used
se to defend itself if cornered by

a coelurosaur. *Heterodontosaurus*
was different from *Lesothosaurus*
because like most other
ornithischians it had cheeks.

It appears that practically all the
known groups of later ornithischian
dinosaur evolved from these early
ornithischians of the Triassic which
ran about on their back legs. Even
the large four-footed ornithischians
such as the stegosaurs (see pages
48–9) and the ceratopians (see pages
66–7) show this two-footed ancestry
because their back legs are much
longer than the front ones.

Ornithopods, rather similar to
Lesothosaurus, seem to have
persisted throughout the Jurassic
Period and into the early part of the
Cretaceous Period.

**Below: At merely 1 metre (3 feet)
long, *Lesothosaurus* was a pocket-
sized dinosaur compared with some
others.**

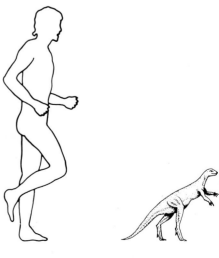

33

Colonizing the sea and air

Dinosaurs were not the only new group of reptiles that appeared in the Triassic Period. Other reptiles took to living in the sea or in the air so that, by the end of the Triassic, reptiles were the dominant large animals in all environments. Their reign lasted until the end of the Cretaceous Period, for about 140 million years.

In the seas, several very distinctive groups of reptile made their appearance, among them the ichthyosaurs, or 'fish-lizards'. The first ichthyosaurs appeared early in the Triassic and were presumably descended from land-living reptiles, but at present we have no idea from which older group they originated.

One of the first ichthyosaurs, *Mixosaurus*, was already very well adapted for living in water: its legs were converted into broad paddles for steering and it had a large fin on its back, while its tail was bent downwards near the end and had a broad fin to drive it through the water. *Mixosaurus* fed on fish, which it caught between its long narrow jaws; these jaws were lined with numerous sharp, pointed teeth. As we have learned earlier (pages 18–19), reptiles normally lay eggs. Ichthyosaurs, however, were so well adapted to living in the sea that they could not have done what marine turtles do today – return to land once a year to lay their eggs. To solve this problem, they gave birth to live young.

Another group to appear in the seas were the placodonts; these were rather stout reptiles with short, powerful legs and a long swimming tail. Two types of placodont had thick bony armour on the upper part of the body. Placodonts seem to have fed largely on shellfish, which they plucked from the sea bed with their peg-like, protruding front teeth. They then cracked open the hard shells of the shellfish by using their back teeth, which were like round, flattened stones. The placodonts seem to have been a very short-lived group, lasting only until the end of the Triassic Period.

Askeptosaurus was a lizard-like marine creature which appeared a this time. It used its long thin tai for swimming and probably fed largely on fish. Alongside these animals lived the nothosaurs; the were very common in the Triassic and grew to 5 metres (16 feet) lon The nothosaurs looked rather lik *Askeptosaurus*, except that they a deeper, flatter, fin-like tail, but two were not directly related.

Several reptiles attempted to colonize the air, with varying success. A family of lizards, calle kuehneosaurs, developed long rib which protruded from the sides o their body and were joined by a web; this allowed them to glide from tree to tree, like the moder 'flying dragons' (*Draco volans*) o South-East Asia. The first true flying reptiles, however, were the pterosaurs, which evolved in the Triassic Period. These were small

Askeptosaurus

Placodus

...tly built reptiles (most of the ...ly pterosaurs were 20–30 ...timetres [8–12 inches] long) ...ose fore-limbs supported large ...hery membranes and functioned ...wings. The arm bones of the ...g were rather longer than usual, ... most of the extensive wing-span ... supported by a single, ...ormously elongated finger (the ...rth). The three other sharp claws ...he hand, and the long toes, were ...d for clinging on to branches or ...ky ledges where the pterosaurs – ...e modern bats – rested and slept. ...e early pterosaurs of the Triassic ...l Jurassic were comparatively ...all, and had long tails and long ...ks lined with sharp teeth. By ...trast, the pterosaurs of the Late ...taceous (see pages 70–71) were ...en large, had very short tails, and ...l lost their teeth.

...ome recently discovered remains ...m Texas indicate that some ...rosaurs had a wing-span of ...rly 15 metres (49 feet). Bigger ...n a small aircraft!

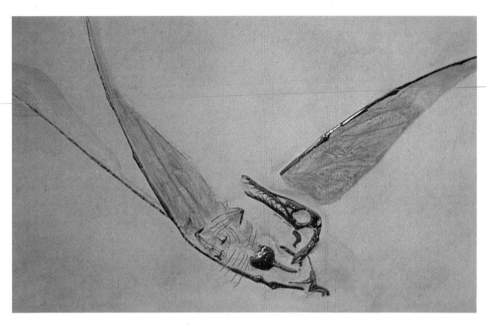

Below: Some of the sea reptiles of the Triassic Period. *Placodus*, with its strong legs and peg-like teeth; *Askeptosaurus*, much more lizard-like in appearance with sharp teeth; and *Mixosaurus*, which somewhat resembled a dolphin in its streamlined shape.

Above: The skeleton of *Rhamphorhynchus*, a type of pterosaur. Notice the splendid preservation of its wing membranes and small kite-shaped tail. Remember that the long wing bones were made up mainly of the fourth finger of its hand.

Mixosaurus

The smallest dinosaurs

Having seen some of the principal kinds of dinosaur that appeared in the Triassic, we can now turn our attention to the Jurassic Period to see how these various groups evolved.

The area of what is now southern Germany, parts of France and Portugal is extremely important for our story. In the latter half of the Jurassic Period, this whole area was covered in shallow tropical lagoons, at the bottom of which was deposited an extremely fine-grained, soft mud. Dead animals which fell to the sea floor were buried in this mud and so became fossilized (see pages 8–9). The mud containing these fossils has now turned to a rock called limestone. When quarried, the limestone occasionally yields beautifully preserved fossils.

By far the most famous fossil to come from these limestones is *Archaeopteryx* (see pages 50–51). But many other wonderfully preserved fossils of the animals that lived in and around these Jurassic lagoons are also known; they include crocodiles, pterosaurs, lizards, many insects, a variety of shellfish and a dinosaur.

The dinosaur, *Compsognathus*, is a **coelurosaur** and therefore similar to *Coelophysis* (see pages 30–31). *Compsognathus* was typical of coelurosaurs in that it had long, spindly legs, grasping hands, a long slender neck and a small head. However, it is remarkable because it is one of the smallest dinosaurs ever found, with a length of about 65 centimetres (2 feet), about the same size as a hen! Since it was so small, and a meat-eater by habit, its prey was probably large insects such as dragonflies, small lizards and perhaps even the occasional grounded pterosaur!

Quite recently a rather interesting new specimen of *Compsognathus* was found near Nice in southern France. It was slightly larger than the earlier specimen – a little over 1 metre (3 feet) long. Although the skeleton of this new *Compsognathus*

was very similar to the first, one scientist thought that he could see the faint impression of the outline of a web of skin between the fingers of the hand. He therefore suggested that this new specimen was a special type of *Compsognathus*, adapted for swimming in the shallow lagoons, where it might catch its prey or possibly escape predators. However, most scientists do not accept that the impression is of a web of skin; they prefer to believe that this specimen was just a large, ordinary *Compsognathus*.

Until recently *Compsognathus* was the smallest dinosaur known. However, in 1977 another dinosaur was found in Argentina, in rocks of latest Triassic or earliest Jurassic age. The skeleton is no larger than that of a thrush and its head is just over 3 centimetres (1¼ inches) long. This specimen has been described by its discoverer, Dr José Bonaparte,

Above: The diminutive *Compsognathus* was only about 65 centimetres (2 feet) long.

Below: *Compsognathus* fossils are known from the Jurassic limeston quarries of Germany and France.

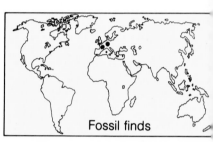

Fossil finds

o believes that it is related to the
up of plant-eating dinosaurs to
ich belong *Plateosaurus* (see
ges 28–9) and the giant sauropods
the Jurassic (see pages 40–43).
Almost as extraordinary as the
covery of this minute dinosaur
s the find, close by, of an almost
fectly preserved egg 2.5
timetres (1 inch) long. It does
t seem possible that this dinosaur
ild have hatched from an egg of
s size, nor could it have laid the
, for it seems to have been a very
ing dinosaur. So we are still
ed with a mystery: to what
mal did the egg belong? Another
all dinosaur is represented by
tial skeletons of *Psittacosaurus*
m Mongolia, preserved in the
ierican Museum of Natural
tory in New York. These are,
wever, very young (baby)
osaurs, rather than naturally
all dinosaurs.

Below: Recently a dinosaur smaller than *Compsognathus* was found in South America; it has been named *Mussaurus* ('mouse-reptile').

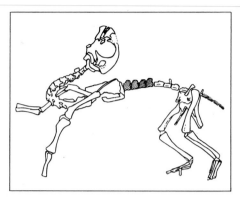

Below: *Compsognathus* has pounced on this pterosaur, which has crash-landed. Although marvellous fliers, pterosaurs were practically helpless on land, since their legs were weak and their wings were very big. Several ichthyosaurs are preserved with pterosaurs in their stomachs.

Above: This fossilized skeleton of *Compsognathus* comes from the same limestone quarries in southern Germany that have yielded beautiful pterosaur fossils and the remarkable fossil of *Archaeopteryx*. Notice how well preserved this skeleton is.

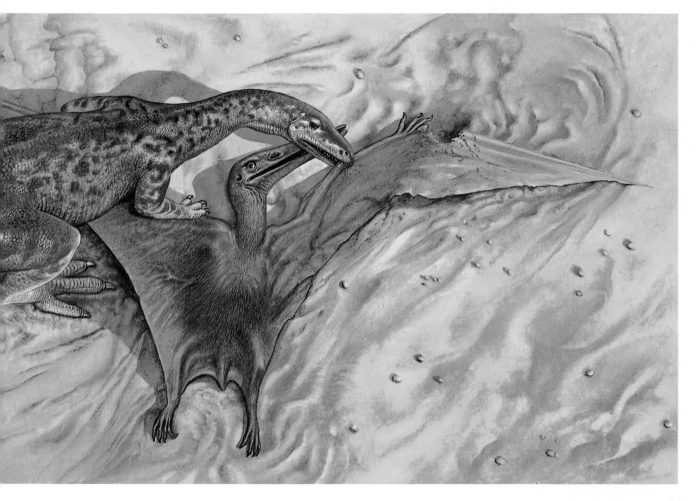

The greedy giant

We have so far discussed two typ
of coelurosaurian dinosaur:
Coelophysis (pages 30–31) and
Compsognathus (pages 36–7). Bu
these small, rather delicate-lookir
animals were not the only types o
flesh-eating dinosaur. At the end
the Triassic Period, the larger and
more powerfully built early
archosaurs like *Ornithosuchus*
disappeared entirely, to be replac
in the next period (the Jurassic) b
even larger, flesh-eating, true
dinosaurs (see pages 30–31) calle
carnosaurs. The carnosaurs diffe
from the coelurosaurs in having
much larger bodies, short powerf
necks and extremely large heads.
They were obviously adapted for
taking much larger prey than wer
the coelurosaurs.

  Allosaurus was one of the large
of the Jurassic carnosaurs (about
10 metres [33 feet] long) and its
fossilized remains have been foun
in North America in rocks of Lat
Jurassic age. This means that it liv
at the same time as *Camptosauru*
(see pages 44–5) and *Stegosaurus*
(see pages 48–9), and it seems lik
that it would have attacked all of
these animals as it pleased. There
even some evidence that *Allosaur*
might have attacked the giant

ropod dinosaurs of this period
h as *Apatosaurus* (see pages
-3) and *Brachiosaurus* (see pages
-41). At one place in North
erica, fossil footprints have
n found, some of which seem to
e been made by a large
ropod walking across a muddy
k and others by a carnosaur
king it (almost certainly
osaurus). Another piece of
vincing fossil evidence, also
nd in North America, consists of
h marks on the tail bones of an
atosaurus, suggesting that a large
nosaur had been feeding on the
ass of this sauropod.
s a meat-eating animal
osaurus would have been
ifyingly efficient. It could not
e run very fast because it was
arge and heavy, weighing up
hree tons, but that did not
ter because the animals it fed
were even larger and heavier.
osaurus would wander off when
sfied, leaving the half-eaten
ass to scavengers.
ne of these opportunists (rather
the modern hyena which waits
cavenge a lion kill) may well
e been *Coelurus*, another
lurosaurian dinosaur. *Coelurus*
d at the same time as

Compsognathus (see pages 36–7)
but was considerably larger, about
2 metres (6½ feet) long. Its main
diet, however, would not have been
the remains of large dinosaurs; it
probably ate lizards, small mammals
and perhaps even pterosaurs.

Apart from *Allosaurus* only three
other Jurassic carnosaurs are known
at all well: *Ceratosaurus*, from
North America, an animal about
half the size of *Allosaurus* and
distinguished by having a peculiar
bump on the top of its snout;
Eustreptospondylus, from England,
which grew to about 4 metres
(13 feet) long; and *Dilophosaurus*
from North America, which had
curious thin crests on its head. Very
few carnosaur skeletons are found
compared with the large numbers of
plant-eaters from this time. This is
probably because there were actually
very few carnosaurs in existence;
each of them needed so much meat
that their numbers were limited by
the availability of their prey. Nature
seems therefore to have controlled
their numbers, maintaining a
constant balance between the
meat-eaters and the plant-eaters.

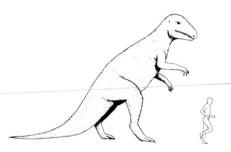

Above: *Allosaurus*, **found in the
western United States (see below),
was 10 metres (33 feet) long.**

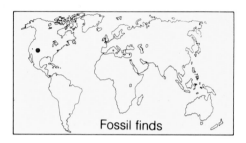

Fossil finds

**Below: The large carnosaur,
Allosaurus (far left) has just feasted
on the carcass of a *Camptosaurus*
that it has killed. Close by, a
few smaller coelurosaurs are
already scavenging the remains
without waiting for *Allosaurus*
to leave.**

The largest dinosaurs

We saw that at the end of the Triassic Period there appeared a group of fairly large plant-eating dinosaurs, such as *Plateosaurus* (see pages 28–9). These were related to the largest land animals that have ever existed, the **sauropod** dinosaurs, which include such giants as *Diplodocus, Apatosaurus* and, one of the biggest of all, the enormous *Brachiosaurus*.

Brachiosaurus grew to a length of about 25 metres (82 feet) and stood 13 metres (43 feet) high! Its bones have been found in East Africa (Tanzania) and North America, in rocks of Late Jurassic age. A complete skeleton of *Brachiosaurus* has been reconstructed in the Museum of Natural Science in East Berlin (see pages 6–7); this demonstrates clearly the extraordinary length of this sauropod's fore-limbs (the name *Brachiosaurus* is Greek for 'arm lizard'). The upper arm bone alone was over 2 metres (6½ feet) long! Most other sauropods (see *Apatosaurus*, pages 42–3) had front legs which were shorter than their back legs, so that their great backs sloped downwards from the hips to the shoulders. However, the reverse was true of *Brachiosaurus*, so that

Right: *Brachiosaurus*, whose remains have been found in Tanzania and North America, may have grown to 25 metres (82 feet) long.

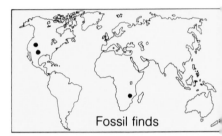

Fossil finds

...ht: The shoulder blade of a ...ture, jokingly called 'Super-...rus', found in North America, is ...n larger than that of *Brachiosaurus*.

...ow: The brachiosaur in the ...ground lays its eggs while the ...ers stay in a group.

the back sloped upwards towards the head. With its sloping back, long neck and small head, *Brachiosaurus* looked very much like a huge overweight giraffe.

How much do we know about the way in which *Brachiosaurus* lived? As it happens, quite a lot. Over the last few years we have been changing our ideas about these animals. Until quite recently (maybe ten years ago) these huge sauropod dinosaurs were thought to have spent all their time in or near water, feeding on the soft, lush water plants. Indeed *Brachiosaurus* seemed in many ways ideally suited to living in this manner. Its enormously heavy body would have been buoyed up by the water, its long neck would have allowed it to walk in deep water, where it could feed in peace (away from the large predators like *Allosaurus*, see pages 38–9); its nostrils were thought to have been placed on a small mound on top of its head, instead of at the tip of the snout, so that it could breathe while its head was almost submerged.

Scientists now doubt these ideas and believe that *Brachiosaurus* spent most of its time on land. For one thing, if *Brachiosaurus* did submerge to a depth of 13 metres (43 feet), its lungs would have been crushed by the enormous water pressure; it could certainly not have drawn air into its lungs. Further, if it had lived in a swampy area, it would very soon become bogged down completely, because its feet were quite small and unsuitable for walking on mud. So it seems that these large sauropods had to live on dry land. Doubts about whether their legs would have been strong enough to support an 80-ton body have now been dismissed.

Brachiosaurus's great height would have been useful to a land animal: like the giraffe today, it could eat the leaves and shoots at the very tops of trees where no other plant-eater could reach them.

Deceptive lizard

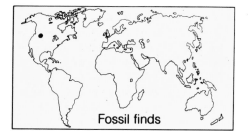

Fossil finds

Left: *Apatosaurus*, **found in the western United States, was 20 metres (66 feet) long.**

Apatosaurus (for a long time called *Brontosaurus*, see pages 74–5) must be one of the best known of all dinosaurs. It was a large, plant-eating **sauropod** that lived in the Late Jurassic. *Apatosaurus* was neither the heaviest sauropod, weighing about 30 tons (much lighter than *Brachiosaurus* which weighed as much as 80 tons), nor was it the longest at 20 metres (66 feet). *Diplodocus*, another well-known sauropod, measured 26 metres (85 feet). Nevertheless, *Apatosaurus* was a typical sauropod.

The head of *Apatosaurus* was quite small and was perched on the end of a long, powerful neck; the trunk was stout and was supported by large pillar-like legs. Unlike *Brachiosaurus*, the front legs were shorter than the back ones so that the back sloped down towards the shoulders. The tail was very long with a thin whip-like end.

Just as with *Brachiosaurus* (see pages 40–41), it is now generally believed that *Apatosaurus* and all other sauropods spent most of their lives on dry land. Their long necks allowed them to feed high up near the tree tops, and they might even have been able to rear up on their back legs so that they could reach

higher still. These sauropods presumably fed on leaves and shoots, which they were able to nip off with their small peg-like teeth. It seems likely that they would have had to feed all day to collect enough food to allow them to grow, and their stomachs would have needed to be enormous to contain such tremendous amounts of plant food properly. Again, like the early plant-eaters (see pages 28–9), the sauropods swallowed stones which they kept in their stomachs for grinding up the tough plant food.

The sauropods were large and slow-moving, which means they would have been tempting prey for flesh-eaters such as *Allosaurus* (see pages 38–9). But *Apatosaurus* may not have been such an easy victim for *Allosaurus*; the long, whip-like tail could have been used to beat off an attacker, and at close quarters

Apatosaurus could rear up on its back legs and try to crush the meat-eater with its front feet. *Apatosaurus* had very large claws on the inner toes of its front feet, which could also have inflicted severe damage on any *Allosaurus* that came too close.

Some footprint tracks of sauropod dinosaurs in North America indicate that sauropods, like plateosaurs, moved about in herds; their young ones stayed near the centre and the larger males around the outside, protecting the herd from attack.

It is very rare to find any sort

of young dinosaur skeleton but in 1922 a baby of the sauropod *Camarasaurus* was discovered. One noteworthy thing about the youngster is that it had a very short neck and quite a large head compared with the fully grown animal.

Although we are now fairly sure that sauropods spent most of their lives on land, there is one remarkable piece of evidence which shows that they were able to swim at times. Another footprint track, again in North America, shows a row of front footprints made by a sauropod that was obviously floating on the surface of the water and walking along the bottom with its front feet only. A little farther on there is one back footprint and then the front footprints change direction. The sauropod must have been using its back feet to steer itself!

Left: This scene from the Upper Jurassic of North America shows an adult and young *Apatosaurus*; they have come down to the cool waterside in the heat of the day to rest and drink. Note how short the neck of the young *Apatosaurus* is compared with that of its parent.

Beaked lizard

All the Jurassic dinosaurs that we have looked at so far have been of the saurischian type; but what of the other group, the ornithischian dinosaurs? In the Late Triassic they were small fleet-footed **ornithopods** such as *Lesothosaurus* (see pages 32–3). We know very little about what happened during the early part of the Jurassic Period, because there are very few rocks anywhere in the world which contain land animals of Early Jurassic age.

However, by the Late Jurassic we find several types of ornithischian dinosaur; some are merely larger versions of the Triassic ornithopods, while others developed a variety of bony plates on their backs (see pages 46–9).

Camptosaurus was like a Triassic ornithopod but larger. Fossils of *Camptosaurus* have been found in North America and England, and it seems to have been a quite common plant-eater of the time; it grew to about 5 metres (16 feet) long and may have weighed about half a ton. As with the earliest ornithischian, or bird-hipped, dinosaurs, the back legs were longer than the front ones and were the main ones used for walking and running. However, although the front legs were quite short, the hands had rather short stubby fingers ending in small hooves instead of claws. This means that the hand (unlike the hand of *Lesothosaurus*, see pages 32–3) could not have been much use for grasping but would have been used mostly for moving on all fours (when walking slowly or feeding from the ground).

We have seen that the teeth of many plant-eating saurischians were very simple peg-like structures, used to pluck off vegetation which was then swallowed whole. To get the nourishment out of such plant food, it is necessary first to crush up the tough leaves and shoots; only then can they be properly digested. In the case of the saurischian dinosaurs this was done with stomach stones (see pages 28–9), but ornithischians,

such as *Camptosaurus*, used a very different method.

The teeth of *Camptosaurus* were neatly arranged in rows in each jaw and were quite thick with rough edges. When the animal bit on its food, these rows of teeth rubbed past each other as the jaws closed and sliced the plants caught between them like a pair of scissors. These dinosaurs were therefore able to break up their food before swallowing it. To be able to do this, without the food falling out of the sides of their mouths, they also needed cheeks. (To see how

important cheeks are in preventi food falling out of your mouth when chewing, try to chew a raw carrot while holding your lips ba as far as you can!) Like all ornithischian dinosaurs, *Camptosaurus* had a bird-like, horny beak at the front of its mouth, which it might have used to nibble off leaves.

Living alongside *Camptosauru* was a smaller ornithischian name *Dryosaurus*. *Dryosaurus* grew to length of 2 metres (6½ feet), and seems to have been merely a smaller, faster-running version o

...mptosaurus. Medium-sized plant-
...rs seem to have been very
...cessful, because different
...nals of this type are found
...oughout the reign of the
...osaurs, until their extinction
...he end of the Cretaceous
...iod.

...he discovery of fossil remains
...Camptosaurus in both North
...erica and England is a
...vincing piece of evidence
...porting the theory that these two
...s were joined together as a
...le land mass during at least part
...he Jurassic Period.

Above: A small herd of
Camptosaurus **are quietly**
browsing on the vegetation. Note
the close-up view of the cheeks of
these animals and also the sharp
horny beak at the front of the
mouth, which was used for
nipping off shoots and leaves.
Notice also the small crater-like
ear drum near the back of the
head.

Right: *Camptosaurus* **measured**
4−5 metres (13−16 feet) long and
its remains have been found in
North America and England.

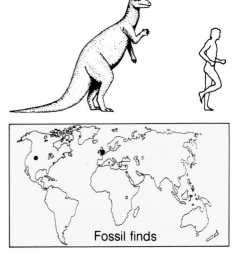

Fossil finds

An unsolved riddle

The one and only well-preserved ornithischian dinosaur that we know of from **early** Jurassic rocks is *Scelidosaurus*, found in England. The skeleton of this dinosaur was embedded in solid limestone. It has only recently been cleaned of this surrounding rock although it was found more than 100 years ago. It will be studied in more detail over the next few years.

Scelidosaurus grew to about 4 metres (13 feet) long and, unlike the previous ornithischians that we have seen, was quite heavily built and walked on all fours. It also had the typical rough-edged, leaf-shaped teeth of a plant-eater.

One of the biggest problems facing the plant-eating dinosaurs was how to avoid being eaten by any of the ferocious meat-eaters. The sauropods were protected to some extent by their enormous size, while amongst the ornithischian dinosaurs different methods of defence were developed. *Lesothosaurus* (see pages 32–3), *Dryosaurus* (see pages 44–5), *Hypsilophodon* (see pages 52–3) and many others were very small, fleet-footed animals that could avoid predators by running away. *Camptosaurus* (see pages 44–5) and *Iguanodon* (see pages 52–3) lived and moved about in herds, trying to discourage the meat-eaters by their sheer numbers. *Triceratops* (see pages 66–7) developed large horns so that it could attack its attackers! *Scelidosaurus* shows us the beginnings of yet another defence method. As can be seen below, the neck, back and tail of *Scelidosaurus* were covered by rows of bony spikes; these would have served as an effective armour plating, rather like that of the modern armadillo of South

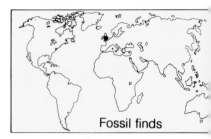

Fossil finds

Below: A large *Megalosaurus* and two younger ones approach *Scelidosaurus*, which has tried to protect its vulnerable underside by drawing itself very close to the ground.

**t: Remains of *Scelidosaurus* are
rare and have been found
on the coast of southern
land in rocks of Early Jurassic

America. *Scelidosaurus*, shielded by this bony armour, could therefore have wandered around fairly safe from attack.

The skin of *Scelidosaurus* would still have been quite flexible, because the bony spikes were all separate. Later, in the Cretaceous Period, another group of ornithischians called the ankylosaurs appeared (see pages 68–9). They may have been relatives of *Scelidosaurus* but we are still not sure. They had developed their armour so much that it formed a solid layer of bony ridges and spikes over the back of the animal, rather like a huge spiky tortoise.

The fact that very few early Jurassic dinosaurs have been found makes it difficult to work out the exact ancestry of the many later Jurassic dinosaurs. Although *Scelidosaurus* should be able to help

us sort out the ancestry of the ornithischian dinosaurs, it actually proves to be a big problem itself. It is quite easy to see how the small, nimble, unarmoured ornithischians of the late Triassic such as *Lesothosaurus* could have eventually evolved into the larger ornithischians of the late Jurassic such as *Camptosaurus*. But it is more difficult to understand how *Scelidosaurus* from the early Jurassic fits into this family tree. It lived after *Lesothosaurus* and long before *Camptosaurus*, so we could logically expect it to have been a fairly small, unarmoured animal with long back legs. However, it is just the opposite of this: a quite large, clumsy, armoured animal that walked on all fours! How does *Scelidosaurus* fit into the story? At the moment we are not sure.

Armour plating or cooling fins?

A dinosaur which is almost as well known as the giant sauropods is *Stegosaurus*, which is also from the late Jurassic of North America; its most characteristic feature was the row of roughly diamond-shaped, bony plates that ran down either side of its backbone.

Stegosaurus was a large animal, about 6 metres (20 feet) long and weighing nearly two tons. It was an ornithischian dinosaur with the characteristic horny beak. It had a rather interesting feature which suggests its possible ancestry: the back legs were almost twice as long as its front ones, just as in those late Triassic ornithischians (see pages 32–3). This suggests that *Stegosaurus*'s ancestors were small animals that ran on their back legs most of the time. As they grew larger, to become more like *Stegosaurus*, they found it more and more difficult to walk on their back legs alone. Instead, they dropped down on to all fours, using their rather short arms as front legs. *Stegosaurus*'s head was tiny in comparison with its body, as was its brain.

Large, rather clumsy-looking plant-eaters such as *Stegosaurus* could have been ideal prey for the large meat-eaters such as *Allosaurus* (see the shadow in the picture, and also pages 38–9). However, *Stegosaurus* had a weapon to fend off possible predators: the end of its tail had two pairs of long, curved bony spikes which it could swing at its enemies with deadly effect. Most scientists believe that the large diamond-shaped plates which ran in two rows down the back of *Stegosaurus* were a form of bony armour, to protect it from attack. However, these plates did not protect the soft sides and belly of the animal (an obvious area for attack by meat-eaters). It has been suggested in the past that the plates were held downwards along the top or the sides of the body to give better protection but, even with these plates folded down, the sides

Below: Two *Stegosaurus* are disturbed by *Allosaurus* (see its shadow). The larger of the two *Stegosaurus* squares itself up against the enemy. Bracing its back legs it starts to swing its tail slowly and menacingly. The huge, sharp spikes on its tail would present quite a threat to the predator.

Above: *Stegosaurus* grew to a length of 6 metres (20 feet).

Below: Remains of *Stegosaurus* have been discovered in the western United States.

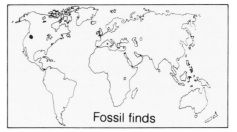

Fossil finds

and belly would still have been exposed. But what were these plates for if they were not used as armour plating?

One exciting suggestion, also made quite recently, is that the plates were used as either solar panels or cooling fins to warm or cool the body, rather like the sails of the sail-back reptiles (see pages 18–19). These bony plates have been thoroughly examined and, when they were cut across, it was discovered that there were large gaps and tunnels running through them – instead of being solid they were rather like a honey comb inside. These gaps and tunnels might have been filled with blood and, if this was so, the plates were most probably used for heating or cooling the blood as it flowed through them. An interesting experiment showed that the shape of these plates was perfect for use as a cooling plate!

So our ideas about dinosaurs, the way they lived and functioned, are constantly changing as new results emerge from the careful studies being carried out. Even well-accepted ideas, like the plates of *Stegosaurus* being armour, are overturned by such work.

49

The first bird

Below: The first bird, *Archaeopteryx*. Note that its backwardly directed inner toe helps it to grip the branch. It has feathers and wings like a bird, but also teeth in its jaws and claws on its wings, reminding us of its reptile ancestry; the long bony tail is less obvious here.

In 1861 the fossilized remains of a fascinating animal were discovered in a stone quarry in southern Germany. They consisted of the almost complete skeleton of a small creature about 35 centimetres (14 inches) long with long arms and legs, a long bony tail and rather bird-like feet (somewhat like an even smaller version of little *Compsognathus*, see pages 36–7). The most amazing thing about this little animal, which had died and fallen into a shallow lagoon in late Jurassic times, was that it had the impressions of feathers preserved around its fore-limbs and tail. These feathers plainly indicated that this animal was an ancient bird, and it was named *Archaeopteryx*, meaning 'ancient wing' in Greek. This tiny creature, no larger than a pigeon, is one of the most famous finds ever made.

The fossil is of especial interest because it appears to show the process of evolution actually occurring. It is widely agreed that birds evolved from reptiles, and *Archaeopteryx* provides proof of this idea: it shows an in-between stage in that evolution, apparently half-way between reptile and bird.

Like a bird, *Archaeopteryx* had wings and feathers, very bird-like feet with a backward-pointed toe for clinging to branches, and a 'wishbone' in its breast (which reptiles do not have).

Like a reptile, however, *Archaeopteryx* had clawed finger

for cutting through flesh, but were ideal for crunching up the hard bodies of insects. *Archaeopteryx* may have caught these in its mouth while in flight or it may have used its feathered wings rather like nets to catch flying insects as it moved about on the ground.

The amazing suggestion has recently been made that birds are really little more than feathered dinosaurs! This proposal has been prompted by the fact that, apart from the fossilized feathers, the skeleton of *Archaeopteryx* is very similar to that of a coelurosaurian dinosaur (see pages 30–31 and 36–7). (One *Archaeopteryx* skeleton was, in fact, wrongly labelled as *Compsognathus* because its feathers had not been preserved.) If this theory is eventually proved correct, and an increasingly large number of palaeontologists think it is, we shall be able to say that the dinosaurs didn't really all die out at the end of the Cretaceous Period (see pages 72–3), because some of their descendants live on today as birds!

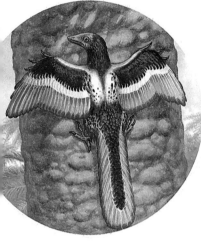

Three views of *Archaeopteryx*: with its wings fully extended and tail feathers fanned out in a gliding position (above); using its clawed wings for clambering up tree trunks to escape from predators (left); and using its wings rather like butterfly nets to catch insects as they fly by (below).

ts hands; a long bony tail (some
ern birds appear to have long
, but they are made of feathers
e, sprouting from the short
py 'parson's nose'); and teeth
s jaws (modern birds have only
y beaks, none has true teeth).
what was *Archaeopteryx*'s way
fe? It had feathers and wings,
ould it have flown like modern
s? For a long time, it was
ght that *Archaeopteryx* might
been able to fly, but only
kly. However, recent research
ests that it may have been able
y as well as, say, modern bats.
its clawed fore-limbs and long
, *Archaeopteryx* would have
a good climber and may have
n to the trees to avoid
ators.
rchaeopteryx probably fed on
cts. Its jaws were lined with
y pointed teeth, which did not
the long, sharp edges necessary

51

Bird feet

In the crumbling cliffs of the southern shores of the Isle of Wight, off southern England, many fossilized fragments of a very well-known dinosaur from the early Cretaceous have been found. They belong to *Iguanodon*, a large (9 metres [29 feet] long) **ornithopod** ornithischian dinosaur, a rather bigger relation of the earlier *Camptosaurus* (see pages 44–5). The bones and teeth of *Iguanodon* were first described in 1825 by Gideon Mantell, a doctor who lived in Lewes in Sussex, England. His

wife, Mary Ann Mantell, first found teeth in 1822 in a pile of rocks at the side of the road; these led him to a stone quarry near Cuckfield in Sussex, where he also found bones. The rocks in which these first finds appeared were, not surprisingly, of the same age as the rocks in the Isle of Wight which later revealed so many *Iguanodon* remains. The teeth, in particular, puzzled Mantell (see pages 10–11). They were 4–5 centimetres (1½–2 inches) long, but, apart from their size, resembled the much smaller

Right: A substantial number of *Iguanodon* and *Hypsilophodon* remains have been found in Western Europe.

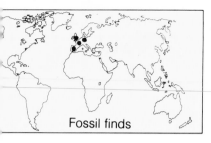

Left: *Iguanodon* grew to 9 metres
feet) long and stood about
etres (16 feet) high on its
k legs; *Hypsilophodon* was
siderably smaller at about
entimetres (27½ inches).

teeth of a Central and South
American lizard called an iguana.
Some years later, in 1841, Richard
Owen, a notorious English
anatomist, re-examined *Iguanodon*
and several other giant fossil reptiles
which had by then been discovered.
He decided to call them all
Dinosauria (from the Greek *deinos*,
meaning 'terrible', and *sauros*,
meaning 'lizard') and so the
dinosaurs were born.

In 1878 the first complete
Iguanodon skeleton was found in a
coal mine in southern Belgium.

Iguanodon was one of the largest
ornithischian plant-eaters of the
time and as such would have been
prey for *Megalosaurus* (see pages
38–9), one of the largest meat-
eaters of this period. *Iguanodon*
probably stayed together in herds
for protection, for several tracks of
Iguanodon footprints have been
found together in southern
England. As with many other
species, herding was probably a
method of protecting young and
female animals from predators.
Fully grown *Iguanodon* would have
been formidable opponents for
Megalosaurus. Not only were they
larger than *Megalosaurus*, but they
also had a dangerous defensive
weapon. Their thumbs were large
bony spikes which grew to about
25 centimetres (10 inches) long;
attached around this spike was the
pointed horny thumb claw, some
40 centimetres (16 inches) long and
slightly curved. In a close tussle
with *Megalosaurus* this huge dagger-
like claw would have been a
devastating weapon.

Alongside *Iguanodon* there lived
another much smaller (up to 2
metres [6½ feet] long) ornithischian
dinosaur with the jaw-cracking
name of *Hypsilophodon*. As we
have already seen (pages 32–3 and
44–5) such small fleet-footed
creatures were found at all times
throughout the reign of the
dinosaurs. One notable characteristic
of *Hypsilophodon* was that its tail
had a very stiff end! This odd
feature might have been used as a
balancing aid, allowing these
animals to change direction or side-
step very quickly; this would make
them extremely difficult to catch,
even by a fast-running predatory
coelurosaur. *Hypsilophodon* was
not the only dinosaur to use its rigid
tail as a balancer (pages 54–55).

**Left: A herd of *Iguanodon* settling
down for the night. Several of the
larger animals stay on guard; close
by (right) a group of *Hypsilophodon*
nestle together in safety.**

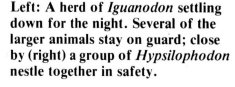

Terrible claw

The remains of a most unusual saurischian dinosaur, called *Deinonychus*, have been found in early Cretaceous rocks in North America. It was something like a **coelurosaur** (see pages 30–31), but was different enough to be placed in a group of its own. We know very little of the smallest meat-eating dinosaurs in early Cretaceous times, most of their remains consisting of small fragments rather than of complete skeletons. The discovery in 1964 of several complete skeletons of *Deinonychus* not only helped us to fill this gap in our knowledge, but also brought to light one of the most extraordinary dinosaurs that ever lived.

Deinonychus was small by dinosaur standards (about 2.5 metres [8 feet] long) with a long balancing tail, long spindly legs and arms and a slender neck; the head was perhaps rather larger than usual in coelurosaurs and the jaws were lined with very sharp teeth. Although most of these characteristics are typical of coelurosaurs, let us look at some of them in more detail to see how *Deinonychus* differs from that group and why it is so unusual.

The tail was indeed long; the vertebrae were surrounded by bundles of bony rods so that the whole tail, except for its base, could be held poker stiff. It could therefore be used as a balancing aid when the creature ran on its back legs.

The legs were long and spindly (for fast running) but the usual bird-like arrangement of toes (see pages 30–31) was strangely altered. The first toe was small and it pointed backwards as usual; the second toe, which bore a huge sickle-shaped claw, was carried clear of the ground and could no longer be used for walking; the third and fourth toes were both in the normal position.

These unusual features of the skeleton suggest that *Deinonychus* was a most remarkable predator.

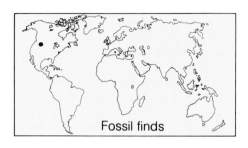

Fossil finds

Above: *Deinonychus* remains have been found in North America.

Below: *Deinonychus* has brought down the defenceless plant-eating dinosaur, *Tenontosaurus*, with a powerful bite to the neck before tearing open its exposed belly.

Above: The sharply clawed *Deinonychus* grew to just under 3 metres (10 feet) long and measured 1 metre (3 feet) high at the shoulder.

Like ordinary coelurosaurs, *Deinonychus* could undoubtedly run very fast to catch its prey. It would grasp it with its long arms and sharply clawed hands and perhaps bite into its neck to bring it down (rather like a lion today catching a zebra). Once brought to the ground, the prey would have been doomed. Keeping a firm grip on its prey, *Deinonychus* would stand on one leg and kick out with the other to rip open the belly of its victim with the sickle-shaped claw; it would then feast until satisfied.

We have explained the unusual foot of *Deinonychus*, but what about the stiffened tail? As with *Hypsilophodon* (see pages 52–3), the rigid tail would have made *Deinonychus* a very agile runner. It could also have been used, rather like a tightrope-walker's pole, for balancing on one leg when slashing at the soft belly of its prey.

The most likely prey for *Deinonychus* would have been medium-sized ornithischian dinosaurs such as *Tenontosaurus* (see below) if it caught them away from the main herd. It is even possible that these relatively small predatory animals hunted together in packs, rather like hunting dogs in Africa today.

Very recently a new and much larger animal of this type has been found in southern England. It is presently being prepared at the British Museum (Natural History) in London.

King of the tyrants

As we approach the end of the Cretaceous Period, we see some of the most extreme developments in the evolution of the dinosaurs.

Among the meat-eaters, the most remarkable of the large **carnosaurs** (see pages 38–9) were the tyrannosaurids, of which *Tyrannosaurus rex* must be the most famous example. *Tyrannosaurus* fossils are rare, but a few skeletons have been discovered in rocks of late Cretaceous age in North America. Very similar relatives of *Tyrannosaurus* are known from other areas, such as *Albertosaurus* from Canada and *Tarbosaurus* from Mongolia.

Tyrannosaurus is the largest predatory dinosaur known: it grew to about 12 metres (40 feet) long and could have reared up on its back legs to a full height of 5 metres (16 feet). Its back legs were enormously long and powerful, as

befitted an animal which weighed up to seven tons. The body was rather short and very stout, the neck short and powerful to support the enormous head (about 1.25 metres [4 feet] long). The body was balanced at the hips by a thick, muscular tail.

One very noticeable and fascinating feature of *Tyrannosaurus* is the extraordinarily short arms, each with only two tiny fingers on the hand. In an early carnosaur such as *Allosaurus* (see pages 38–9),

the arms were not very long, but they were powerful and each hand had three sharp claws which could be used for tearing flesh. What use then had the tiny arms of *Tyrannosaurus*? They were too small to be used for grappling with prey and, unless *Tyrannosaurus* twisted its head far to one side, they could not even reach its mouth. A recent suggestion that seems quite likely is that the arms were used as anchors (to prevent the body from sliding

vards when the animal was trying
et up). When these animals
ed, they probably did so flat
heir bellies. When they
ted to stand up again, they
ld tuck their back legs under
n and try to heave themselves
However, it seems likely, from
way that the body was balanced,
as *Tyrannosaurus* straightened
egs it would simply slide
vards with its chin on the
und! So its arms may have been
l to take a firm grip on the

ground and prevent its body from
sliding forwards when it tried to
stand up. Although lacking
substantial proof, this suggestion
provides some sensible function for
those otherwise ridiculously short
arms.

Tyrannosaurus probably preyed
upon a variety of plant-eating
dinosaurs, including the horned
ceratopians (see pages 66–7) and
duck-billed dinosaurs (see pages
60–61), both of which were quite
common in the late Cretaceous. Its

huge head had very large, powerful
jaws which were lined with sharp
teeth, used for stabbing and slicing.
The jaw joint was of a special type
so that the mouth could be opened
wide, allowing *Tyrannosaurus* to
swallow huge chunks of meat.

One of the very few groups of
animal that were relatively immune
to attacks by this terrifying predator
were the ankylosaurs (see pages
68–9), large tank-like ornithischian
dinosaurs with very thick armour
plating.

**Left: An imaginary reconstruction
showing a young *Chasmosaurus*
caught by *Tyrannosaurus*.
Discovering the loss of their
youngster, the parents charge to
its defence.**

**Below: *Tyrannosaurus* grew to up
to 12 metres (40 feet) long.**

Fossil finds

**Above: *Tyrannosaurus* remains
have been found in America.**

Ostrich dinosaurs

The flesh-eating dinosaurs of the Cretaceous included not only the large, heavily built carnosaurs such as *Tyrannosaurus* (see pages 56–7), but also smaller, slimmer, long-legged **coelurosaurs**. Some of these coelurosaurs looked much like those of earlier periods (see pages 30–31 and 36–7); but more usually the Cretaceous coelurosaurs were toothless descendants of those earlier forms, a good example being *Ornithomimus* from North America and Asia.

The name *Ornithomimus* means 'bird imitator', and indeed these animals did look remarkably bird-like. A typical *Ornithomimus* was about the same size as an ostrich today, though they were sometimes much larger; they were also similar to ostriches in appearance, with very long slender back legs, a long neck and a small head. The feet were three-toed and very bird-like. The long tail ensured that the body was balanced at the hips, enabling the animal to run on its back legs. *Ornithomimus* was different in this respect from the ostrich which, like all birds, is able to balance on two legs, even though it hasn't got a tail, because of the arrangement of its leg bones. The fore-limbs of *Ornithomimus* were not shortened at all; the hand had three long, clawed fingers which were obviously used for grasping, and the inner finger was twisted inwards (rather like our own thumbs) so that small objects could be held very firmly in a vice-like grip.

The head of *Ornithomimus* was similar to a bird's head: very small, light and with large eyes. The similarity to a bird, however, went even further because these coelurosaurs, unlike all other

Above: A typical *Ornithomimus* grew to about 4 metres (13 feet) l

Below: Ornithomimids are know from Asia and western North America; their fossils are found rocks of Cretaceous age.

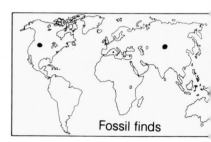

Fossil finds

Right: We are not sure on what these peculiar toothless ornithomimids fed. Perhaps they gave up the meat-eating habit of their ancestors and took to eating fruits and berries.

osaurs, had lost all their teeth.
e jaws were slender and weak and
e probably equipped with a
ny bill.

he odd combination of
aracteristics found in these
rich-like dinosaurs – long slender
s for fast running, long arms
h grasping hands, and a weak,
thless jaw – has made it difficult
guess their way of life. It has
n suggested that they fed largely
eggs, stolen from the nests of
er dinosaurs. After all, teeth are
needed for egg-eating since the

ove right: The slender long legs
Ornithomimus suggest that it
s a very fast-running dinosaur.
re it is shown chasing insects.

ow: *Ornithomimus* may have
n eggs stolen from other
osaurs.

shell can be broken with the horny
beak; the hand would have been of
great use for holding the eggs; and
the ability to run fast would have
been necessary to avoid the enraged
dinosaurs whose eggs they had
stolen! Another suggestion is that
the 'ostrich dinosaurs' would have
fed on almost anything and
everything that was available. Like
their ancestors, they probably fed
on lizards and small mammals,
which they could catch with their
grasping hands. However, they may
also have taken to eating fruits and

perhaps even young shoots and
leaves.

Some interesting calculations
have been made by measuring the
leg bones of 'ostrich dinosaurs'
and comparing them with those
of the living ostrich. The results
seem to suggest that these
dinosaurs could probably have
run at least as fast as an ostrich,
maybe 80 kph (50 mph)! They were
probably the fastest dinosaurs that
ever lived. However, we can never
actually prove that they could run
this fast.

Duck~billed dinosaurs

The hadrosaurs or duck-billed dinosaurs, descendants of the plant-eating **ornithopods** of the early Cretaceous such as *Iguanodon* (see pages 52–3), lived in North and South America, Europe and Asia during late Cretaceous times.

These animals seem to have been very numerous, for many fossil skeletons are known. As can be seen below, the structure of the head varied enormously within this group, yet the bodies of them all were almost identical. The animal was usually about 10 metres (33 feet) long and, in general, was much like *Iguanodon*. The long back legs were three-toed, the toes ending in broad hooves rather than claws. The fore-limbs, as usual, were shorter than the legs, but the hands had lost their thumbs altogether. Of the remaining fingers on each hand, the first two had small hooves and the other two were slender, grasping fingers. It would seem from this combination of fingers that the hand was used sometimes for walking and sometimes for grasping.

When we consider the most extraordinary part of a hadrosaur, the head, two areas are of particular interest: the jaws and teeth, and the bizarre crests. The jaws and teeth show an extremely complicated arrangement for mincing plant food. The teeth were arranged in each jaw in what are

Above: An impression of the skin of an ornithopod dinosaur showing details of its scaly surface.

Below: This fossilized jaw of a hadrosaur shows the remarkable batteries of teeth. Small and diamond-shaped, they fit together neatly. The teeth were worn down at the top and new teeth gradually grew up to replace them.

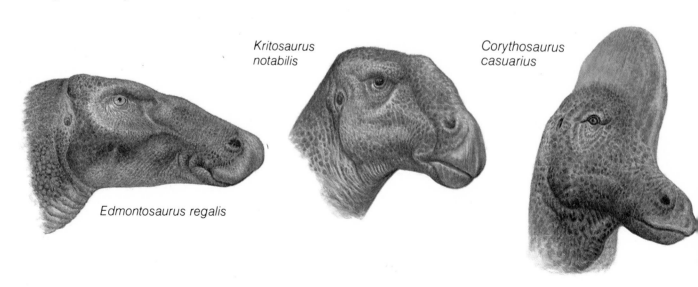

Kritosaurus notabilis

Corythosaurus casuarius

Edmontosaurus regalis

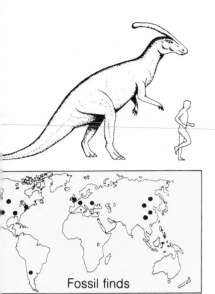

Fossil finds

**ove: Most hadrosaurs grew to
etres (30 feet) long. Their
ains have been discovered in
rth and South America, Asia,
tain and Europe. One Chinese
rosaur, *Shantungosaurus*, is
metres (49 feet) long, by far the
gest in the world.**

**ow: Duck-billed dinosaurs
l extraordinary crests. These
mples illustrate the main types
head shape.**

called 'batteries'. Each battery contained several hundred teeth, all of which fitted neatly together to form a long grinding surface, rather like a carpenter's file. When the jaws were closed, the batteries rubbed past each other, and any plant food caught between the surfaces was ground into tiny fragments. A large muscular tongue was used to position the food between the batteries, while fleshy cheek pouches prevented the food from falling from the sides of the mouth. A broad, horny beak at the front of the jaws was used to nibble off leaves and shoots. For many years it was believed that hadrosaurs used their beaks rather as ducks do today, for dabbling in water, and this was the reason for the popular name, 'duck-billed' dinosaurs. However, it is now generally believed that they spent most of their time on land.

The crests that are found on the heads of many (but not all) types of hadrosaur are highly characteristic, and there has been much argument

as to what they were for. At one time the long tube-like crest of *Parasaurolophus* was thought to have been used as a snorkel, allowing the animal to breathe while feeding with its nose underwater. Unfortunately, there is no air hole at the far end of the crest! It was also suggested that the crest might have been used as an air reserve for diving. But not enough air could have been trapped in the crest to have been of any real use.

There have recently been some more sensible suggestions. The first was that the crests contained a very elaborate series of air passages, which gave the hadrosaurs an improved sense of smell. The second was that the hollow chambers were used as special sound-producing pipes, rather like the pipes of a trumpet or French horn, enabling the hadrosaurs to bellow at each other, which could have been useful for attracting mates or warning off intruders.

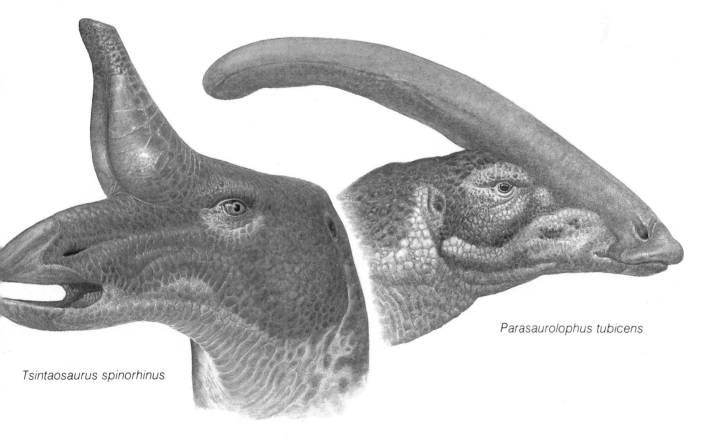

Tsintaosaurus spinorhinus

Parasaurolophus tubicens

Bone heads

One very curious group of ornithischian dinosaurs from the late Cretaceous Period is the **pachycephalosaurs**, a name which means literally 'thick-headed lizards'. They seem to have grown to 2–8 metres (6–26 feet) long, and several different types can be recognized according to how much the skull has thickened. The great thickening of the top of the head in these animals is solid bone and not at all like the hollow crests of the duck-billed dinosaurs (described on pages 60–61). The rest of the skeleton is very similar to that of some of the smaller, lightly built ornithopod dinosaurs of the early Cretaceous (see *Hypsilophodon* on pages 52–3). Indeed some small fragments of a possible ancestor of the pachycephalosaurs have been found in rocks of early Cretaceous age in southern England, practically alongside those of *Hypsilophodon*.

Although the existence of these dinosaurs has been known for many years, it is only recently that people have begun to question the possible purpose of the peculiarly thickened skull roof. One suggestion is that it enabled the male animals to butt each other with their heads, when fighting over females. Indeed, two rams butting today are probably behaving very much like two male pachycephalosaurs over 70 million years ago. Male animals would occasionally separate off from the main herd, face and then charge each other, lowering their heads just a few moments before they collided head on with a loud crack. The weaker of the two would then back away and return to the main herd. Such head-to-head ramming would have been most common during the mating season when the males were competing for females. Such contests of strength, which are found among many herding animals today, determine which is the largest and strongest animal, and therefore the best able to defend and lead the rest of the herd in

Above: *Pachycephalosaurus* might have grown to 6 metres (20 feet) long.

Below: Remains of animals of this type have been found at the sites indicated.

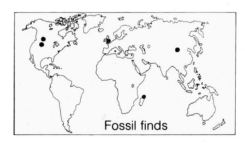

Fossil finds

Above right: Two *Pachycephalosaurus* charge each other using the thick roofs of their skulls as weapons.

Right: A clue to a possible reason for the pachycephalosaurs' thickened skulls was found in the behaviour of mountain sheep.

times of danger. We can only assume that pachycephalosaurs lived in a herd, for we have no direct evidence to prove it.

It may be that we have not found many pachycephalosaur skeletons because most of them lived in upland or hilly areas where fossils are rarely preserved. The reason for their rather lonely life, far from the areas where most of the predators lived, was that they were very vulnerable. They were generally quite small (*Pachycephalosaurus* is the only large pachycephalosaur known), not very fleet-footed and lacked any good defensive weapons. They would have been ideal prey for the fearsome flesh-eaters, which were extremely numerous in the late Cretaceous.

Frilled dinosaurs

The last of the ornithischian dinosaur groups to appear were the well-known **ceratopian** dinosaurs, including the famous *Triceratops* (see pages 66–7). The whole life-span of this group appears to be confined to the late Cretaceous. Among the ceratopians' most characteristic features were a peculiar hooked beak (like a parrot's), a frill of bone at the back of the head, and usually one or more large horns. Most ceratopians were sturdily built, four-footed plant-eaters; they had relatively short front legs, which suggests that their ancestors were two-footed.

The ancestry of the ceratopians is not at all clear, but one of their ancestors may have been the early Cretaceous *Psittacosaurus*; this was a fairly small (2 metres [6½ feet] long) dinosaur which has been found in Mongolia. *Psittacosaurus* had the parrot-like beak of ceratopians but had neither the frill nor the horns. It was a sturdy animal that walked mainly on its back legs, but could also have walked on all fours when necessary. *Psittacosaurus* may itself have been a descendant of some small early

Above: Several nest sites of *Protoceratops* have been found in Mongolia. These show that the eggs were laid in a ring-like arrangement.

Below: A *Protoceratops* hatchling emerging from an egg.

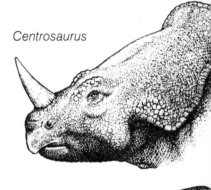

Centrosaurus

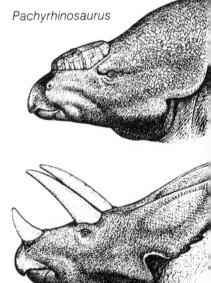

Pachyrhinosaurus

Pentaceratops

Cretaceous ornithopods such as *Hypsilophodon* (see pages 52–3).

The ceratopians may have evolved the parrot-like beak and frill at the back of the head in order to take advantage of some new, tougher plants that appeared on Earth some time around the middle of the Cretaceous Period. The beak would have been a very effective tool for cutting up tough plants, and the frill probably developed originally for the attachment of larger muscles, which would have allowed the ceratopians to chop up their food more easily.

The first typical ceratopian dinosaur was *Protoceratops* (see below). Like *Psittacosaurus*, it was found in Mongolia in large numbers, ranging in size from very young ones to adults about 2 metres (6½ feet) long. Several nests of eggs were also discovered. *Protoceratops* had the typical parrot-like beak of the ceratopian and also the well-developed frill, spreading out over the back of the neck. The final feature, the horns, had not yet appeared; nevertheless, the top of the snout of *Protoceratops* (where one of the horns should have been) was high and arched as if to support a horn, and in some individuals there were rough patches over the eyes where another pair of horns is often found in later ceratopians (see pages 66–7).

Unlike *Psittacosaurus*, *Protoceratops* was quite heavily built; its tail was shorter and could not have been used to balance the body at the hips, which means that it must have been completely four-footed.

Vulnerable though animals such as these small *Protoceratops* must have been, they somehow survived to give rise to many larger ceratopians. Their descendants, together with the duck-billed dinosaurs (see pages 60–61), dominated the lowland areas of the world until the end of the Cretaceous Period.

t: Frilled dinosaurs are acterized by the shape of frill or the number and ngement of the horns, ranging n Pachyrhinosaurus with a y thickening on top of its skull Pentaceratops with three large ns and pointed cheek bones.

Above: A fossilized struggle between a *Protoceratops* and the flesh-eating *Velociraptor*.

Below: A restoration of the scene above showing more clearly how the two animals battled before dying and becoming fossilized.

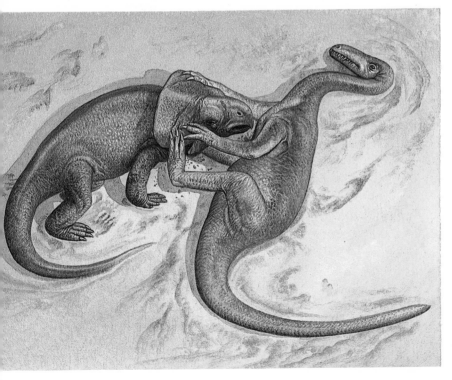

Three horns

Right: The normally peaceful plant-eating ornithischian dinosaur *Triceratops*, with its huge brow horn and nose horns, probably was more than a match for any predator.

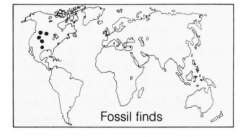

Above: *Triceratops* was about 7 metres (23 feet) long.

Below: Fossils of *Triceratops* were found in western North America.

Fossil finds

Immediately after the appearance of *Protoceratops* (see pages 64–5), the **ceratopian** group of dinosaurs began to evolve very rapidly. This produced a surprisingly large variety of ceratopians (at least 17 distinct types!) over the remaining 25 million years or so of the Cretaceous Period.

Very soon the small, vulnerable, and probably timid *Protoceratops* was replaced by several much larger types. Some had particularly large frills, and others developed a very large head and a rather smaller frill. *Centrosaurus* (see page 64) was one of those early, larger ceratopians; it grew to about 5 metres (16½ feet) long and was very sturdily built. It resembled the present-day rhinoceros, because on its nose it had developed a large bony horn. As well as the nose horn there were two very small ridges, one over each eye, that were the beginnings of the brow horns found in later ceratopians. These large ceratopians probably lived in the lush lowland areas where there was plenty of food. With their large horns they were formidable animals well able to defend themselves against large **carnosaurs**.

Centrosaurus had a quite short frill, while another ceratopian, *Chasmosaurus*, had a very long frill (see pages 56–7) with pointed ed *Chasmosaurus* had also develop large brow horns, as well as the nose horn, and was even better able to defend itself than was *Centrosaurus*, although, as we h seen (pages 56–7), most of these horned dinosaurs would have be preyed upon by the giant **tyrannosaurids**.

he largest of all the ceratopian
osaurs was *Triceratops*, which
to a length of over 7 metres
feet) and may have weighed as
h as five or six tons. Along with
osaurus and *Tyrannosaurus*,
eratops must be one of the best
wn of all dinosaurs.
riceratops was one of the last of
ceratopian dinosaurs to evolve.

The massive frill covered its neck
and shoulders, and its head was
about one third of the length of the
whole body. The huge frill
undoubtedly protected the neck and
shoulders of *Triceratops* from
attacks by the giant meat-eaters,
and as a shield in head-to-head
wrestling matches between
males – like stags in the rutting

season. Behind the sharp, hooked
beak used for slicing off leaves and
twigs the jaws were lined with rows
of extremely sharp teeth which
locked together to form continuous
cutting edges, just like scissor
blades. The sharp cutting edges
meant that *Triceratops*' jaws could
easily chew up the tough, woody
plants on which it fed.

Armoured dinosaurs

As we have seen earlier in this book, the ornithischian dinosaurs developed a number of different defences to avoid being killed by the flesh-eating saurischians. Some became fast runners, some grew very large, others lived in herds, some perhaps sought refuge in the water and still others developed fearsome defensive weapons (see pages 66–7). However, the early Jurassic dinosaur, *Scelidosaurus* (see pages 46–7), developed a type of bony armour plating that could resist the sharp teeth of the flesh-eaters.

In the late Jurassic and Cretaceous Periods, a group of dinosaurs called **ankylosaurs** appeared; they may have been relatives of *Scelidosaurus*. The ankylosaurs had developed a much more complete armour than had *Scelidosaurus*. Some were protected by a simple shield of bony armour which stretched across the head, over the back and down to the end of the tail; others, however, had more effective armour plating which was supplemented by sharp bony spikes in certain areas.

In the early part of the Cretaceous Period the ankylosaur *Hylaeosaurus* lived in what is now southern England. *Hylaeosaurus* was protected by bony spikes which ran along its neck, shoulders, back and down its tail, as well as by a broad flat shield of bony armour over its hips.

In the late Cretaceous there lived a variety of ankylosaurs, especially in North America and Asia; they were all massive tank-like animals. An example of these later ankylosaurs is *Euoplocephalus*. It grew to about 6 metres (20 feet) long and probably weighed four or five tons. The armour plating of this animal was very well developed over the whole of the top of its body; at regular intervals across the smooth armour there were low, blunt spikes, which would have made it very difficult for a flesh-eater to get a grip on the body of *Euoplocephalus*.

Some ankylosaurs, it would s merely dug their toes into the ea and held themselves flat on the ground when attacked. Their th armour made them practically immune to the teeth and claws c the carnosaurs. The armour plat was so well developed in some ankylosaurs that even the eyelid had bony plates in them. These acted like the steel shutters on windows. In fact a carnosaur co have succeeded in killing and ea an ankylosaur only if it managec turn the ankylosaur on to its bac since the belly area was complet unprotected.

One group of ankylosaurs, including *Euoplocephalus*, were only well armoured but also had unusual defensive weapon. At th end of the tail a number of bony plates were welded together to fe a large rounded club. This heavy tail club could be swung at the le and feet of any attacking meat-eaters, giving them an extremely painful blow and perhaps even breaking a leg.

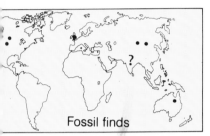

...ove: *Euoplocephalus* grew to a
...gth of 6 metres (20 feet).

**...ow: Remains of armoured
...osaurs have been discovered at
...e sites.**

Fossil finds

**...ht: A fossil impression of the
...** of *Euoplocephalus*.

...ow: *Euoplocephalus*, with its
**...regnable armour coating and tail
...b, would most often have been
...re than a match for these large
...nnosaurs.**

Reptiles of the sea and air

During the Cretaceous Period, while the dinosaurs ruled the land, some very different types of reptile dominated the seas and the air. Most were descendants of the reptiles that had lived in the sea and air during late Triassic times (see pages 34–5), but there was one group of newcomers.

In the seas, one of the dominant groups of reptiles was the plesiosaurs, some of which had remarkably long swan-like necks and small heads. This group had short, squat bodies, short, pointed tails and long, diamond-shaped flippers instead of legs. Their teeth were sharp and pointed, and we can presume that they fed mainly on fishes. The bony fishes of the Cretaceous Period were rather like those of today, being highly manoeuvrable and much faster swimmers than the long-necked

plesiosaurs. Plesiosaurs swam rather slowly; all four 'legs' were used like paddles which they flapped up and down in the water, rather like the wings of a bird, so that they 'flew' along gracefully. They would have been able to catch the fast little bony fishes by flicking their heads out very quickly, on their long necks, into a shoal of fishes as they swam past. Some plesiosaur fossils have been found with both pterosaur and fish bones in their stomachs, suggesting that they either caught the pterosaurs on the wing while they were gliding over the waves or picked up those that had somehow crashed into the sea.

Another very formidable group of sea reptiles (the new arrivals on the scene) were the mosasaurs, gigantic lizards that had left the land and gone back to living in the sea at some time in the early Cretaceous. Like the plesiosaurs,

mosasaurs had paddles for swimming, but they also used the long tail to help drive them thro the water. These ferocious anim fed on most large sea-going creatures, including plesiosaurs and the giant sea turtles of the time. Youngsters like the one below may even have tried leaping for some of the large *Pteranodon* as they soared over the wave tops.

The pterosaurs were still quite

Below: Some *Elasmosaurus* (lon necked plesiosaurs) crane their le necks out of the water while cha a shoal of fish.

mmon in coastal areas. They were
ch larger than in Jurassic times,
example, the toothless, crested
ranodon (see right) had a wing
n of up to 7 metres (23 feet).
ewhere, however, the birds were
dually replacing the pterosaurs
ause birds could fly much better.
ranodon would have spent much
ts time gliding slowly over the
ves, scooping up fish with its
g pointed beak.
Quetzalcoatlus, a giant pterosaur
he late Cretaceous of Texas,
y even have been a carrion
der, scavenging the carcasses of
d dinosaurs.

Below: *Pteranodon* might have had
a pouch beneath their beaks in
which, as they soared above the
waves, they could collect fishes.

Above: A young *Mosasaurus* has
leapt out of the water, trying to
catch a pterosaur.

Why did dinosaurs disappear ?

At the very end of the Cretaceous Period, about 65 million years ago, a puzzling thing happened. On the land, the dinosaurs all disappeared without trace. In the air, the same thing happened to the pterosaurs (see pages 70–71); and in the seas, the ichthyosaurs, plesiosaurs, mosasaurs (see pages 70–71) and a whole variety of shellfish vanished entirely. What could have happened to cause the disappearance not only of the dinosaurs but also of so many other groups of animals? Nobody can give a satisfactory answer to this mystery. But let us take a brief look at some of the attempts that have been made to solve the riddle.

Many of the theories for the late Cretaceous extinctions concern the dinosaurs alone and do not account for the other groups. This approach to the problem seems rather unwise. These theories range from the ridiculous (beings from outer space killing off all the dinosaurs!) to more sensible suggestions (the inability of plant-eating dinosaurs to eat many of the new kinds of woody plant which appeared towards the end of the Cretaceous Period). However, theories based only on the problems caused by the changes in plant life can also be rejected, for dinosaurs, the **ceratopians** (see pages 64–7) and the **hadrosaurs** (see pages 60–61), had successfully adapted their teeth especially to cope with the new plants. Another suggestion made by a scientist at Kew Gardens, England, is that the new plants poisoned the dinosaurs, which were unable to taste the plant poisons called alkaloids; but just because modern tortoises have a poor sense of taste, does it follow that dinosaurs must have had the same?

Other theories concern dinosaur eggs. Perhaps the dinosaurs were killed off by the small mammals (see pages 18–19) which ate all their eggs; or perhaps the eggs were too thick for the young to break out of. On the other hand, a recent study has suggested that their shells were too thin, implying that there were not enough minerals in the egg-shell to allow the embryo dinosaur to develop properly. Do any of these theories also explain the disappearance of the air and sea animals? The answer must be that they do not!

Today there are two general theories which have been put forward as attempts to explain the mass extinctions at the end of the Cretaceous Period. The first of these could be described as proposing some form of *cosmic catastrophe*. From this point of view, the extinctions are regarded as happening very suddenly right at the end of the Cretaceous Period, and therefore something very dramatic must have happened. Various proposals for a dramatic end have been made. For example, perhaps a star exploded very close to our solar system and bathed the Earth in deadly radiation. An interesting but unprovable idea. A much more popular proposal, however, is that made by Luis Alvarez and colleagues in the United States. T theory suggests that a giant meteorite 10 kilometres (6 miles) across collided with the Earth, causing a gigantic explosion as it punched a hole in the Earth's cru The huge explosion would have thrown large quantities of dust a water vapour high into the atmosphere where it formed a thi blanket, blotting out the sun for several months at least. The effec this dust-blanket would have been to completely disrupt plant and animal life on Earth, all of which depends ultimately on sunlight. I support of this theory, Alvarez h discovered a rare element, named *Iridium*, concentrated in clay sediments formed at the very end the Cretaceous Period. He claims that this element could only have

Below: A world-wide change in climate, bringing much cooler weather at the end of the Cretaceous, could have killed off the dinosaurs.

ome from an extra-terrestrial
ource such as a meteorite. There
re many supporters of this theory
t the moment.

There is, however, an alternative
oint of view advocated by other
cientists interested in this problem.
his is that the extinctions were not
he result of such a dramatic event,
ut happened gradually. This might
e called the *gradual climatic
hange* theory. The theory proposes
hat by the end of the Cretaceous
eriod the climatic conditions
orld-wide had deteriorated badly.
n the Jurassic and early Cretaceous
he climate world-wide appears to
ave been very warm and mild all
ear round. However, by the end of
he Cretaceous the climate had
ecome decidedly seasonal with
ild summers and cool or perhaps
old winters. These changes affected
he plants (which seem to have
ecome more hardy types) and the
nd animals (by favouring those
hich were small and could

hibernate over winter if 'cold-
blooded' [amphibians and reptiles]
or keep themselves warm by being
'warm-blooded' [birds and
mammals]), leaving the dinosaurs
which could do neither to go
extinct. The change in climate could
also have had a dramatic affect on
sea-creatures. Planktonic animals
and plants are sensitive to
temperature change and a
temperature drop could have caused
the massive extinctions of plankton
seen at the close of the Cretaceous.
The disappearance of many
planktonic species would have
disrupted food-chains leading in
turn to the disappearance of many
sea-creatures. What caused the
climatic change? One obvious
candidate is the movement of
continents (Plate Tectonics). During
the Jurassic and Cretaceous Periods,
the continents were pretty well
clustered together around the
equator when the climate was mild
and non-seasonal. Toward the end

**Above: A recent theory explaining
the disappearance of the dinosaurs
is that a star exploded near our
solar system, exposing animal life
to deadly radiation.**

of the Cretaceous, the continents
had moved slowly northward and
were separated by seaways. These
changes could have produced the
more seasonal conditions which
caused the extinctions.

So, which of these two theories is
correct? The simple answer is that
no-one really knows. Each group
continues to search for new facts to
support one view or the other. This
search may lead to completely new
theories, or to support one, rather
than the other. It is even possible
that these opposite views may be
reconciled: perhaps the dinosaurs
(and other groups) gradually
declined with worsening climatic
conditions toward the end of the
Cretaceous before being pushed to
extinction by a meteorite impact!

73

Dinosaurs and 'warm blood'

For over a decade now, there has been considerable debate over the issue of whether or not dinosaurs were 'warm-blooded'. By 'warm-blooded' we really mean animals such as mammals and birds living today which are able to generate their own body heat internally and to keep warm, even in quite cold conditions. The technical term used to describe this ability is *endothermy* (which means literally 'inside heat'). This particular way of living can have distinct benefits. For example, *endotherms* living in cold or variable climates can remain active all the year round. However, there is also a cost associated with endothermy — the animal has to eat a great deal because most of its food is used simply to create heat.

These 'warm-blooded' or *endothermic* animals can be compared to others such as amphibians and reptiles; these animals are not able to create body heat in the same way as mammals and birds. These are so-called 'cold-blooded' or *ectothermic* (literally 'outside-heat') creatures which remain cold and inactive on cold days. They rely on the sun to warm their bodies and bring them up to a proper working temperature. However, because they do not burn up food to keep their bodies warm they do not require nearly so much food as endotherms.

Knowing that there are these two ways of controlling body temperature, it was assumed that dinosaurs, since they were reptiles, must also be *ectotherms* or 'cold-blooded' just like their living cousins. This view has been challenged strongly over the last few years by several people who believe that dinosaurs may have been 'warm-blooded' like mammals and birds today. A few of the arguments are explained below.

The fossil record: mammals versus dinosaurs

A puzzling observation from the fossil record is that although mammals are much more successful than reptiles today, they have not always been so. Mammals first appeared on Earth about 205 million years ago (refer back to time-chart) at about the same time as the first dinosaurs. Yet despite the present-day success of mammals it was the dinosaurs that rose to dominate the land for 140 million years. The mammals persisted as small, nocturnal (active at night) shrew-like creatures through the reign of the dinosaurs and only r to dominance after the dinosaur had gone extinct.

To explain this peculiar histor some scientists have proposed that dinosaurs just *had* to be endothermic to have dominated mammals for so long. Others ha attempted to explain the rise of

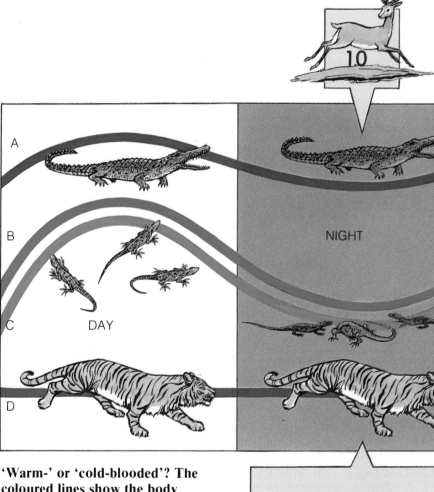

'Warm-' or 'cold-blooded'? The coloured lines show the body temperatures of different animals, in relation to the outside temperature (line B). For very small 'cold-blooded' animals, body temperature (line C) rises and falls exactly with the air temperature, and they only need to eat small amounts.

A 'warm-blooded' tiger's body temperature stays the same (line D). To keep up body heat, the tiger needs to eat ten times as much as a

dinosaurs in terms of their ...elopment of more effective ways ...valking and running; or as a ...lt of climatic change to hot ...ditions favouring the dinosaurs ...ead of the mammals. ...Jnfortunately there is no space to ...sider all the arguments in detail ...ve shall just touch on a few of ...other suggestions concerning ...rm-blooded' dinosaurs.

DAY

...-blooded animal of the same ...— like a crocodile. ...he crocodile, however, is many ...es bigger than the small 'cold- ...oded' reptiles and has more flesh ...fat to insulate it. Its body ...perature (line A) doesn't rise ...fall to the same extremes with ...t and day. ...inosaurs may have followed the ...e pattern — their great body ...keeping their body temperature ...ost as level as that of a 'warm- ...oded' animal.

Predator/prey ratios

As we said earlier, 'warm-blooded' animals need to take in much greater amounts of food than 'cold-blooded' animals because up to 90 per cent of all the food that is eaten is used to create heat. Thus, while a 'cold-blooded' crocodile might need to eat the equivalent of 10 zebra/antelope in a year, a similar-sized tiger may need to eat about 100 zebra/antelope.

Knowing this, some palaeontologists have counted the numbers of predatory and prey dinosaurs in the fossil record. The results suggested that dinosaur predators were very few in number and their prey were very abundant. This *suggests* that at least predatory dinosaurs may indeed have been 'warm-blooded'. Unfortunately, however, there are all sorts of problems with this type of work. Were the dinosaurs being counted actually living together? Are the numbers accurate enough to merit these conclusions? In addition it now appears that *big* predators seem to eat similar quantities of food whether they are 'warm-' or 'cold-blooded'.

Sophisticated dinosaurs(!)

Another line of investigation has been to look at the complexity of some dinosaurs. *Deinonychus*, for example (pages 54–5), is an extremely complex dinosaur; it was built to run very quickly, has a special balancing tail, large eyes and a large brain. Does this really look as though it lived the slow, plodding existence of a tortoise/turtle? The answer must be No! But does this in turn mean that it was highly active and by implication 'warm-blooded'? The answer has to be: we do not know for sure, but it seems quite a strong possibility.

Bone histology (structure)

Many years ago, it was discovered that very thin, polished sections of dinosaur bones looked remarkably like the bones of some living mammals, such as a cow. Both had lots of thin channels for blood running through them. By contrast, reptile bone has very few channels in it and shows clear, yearly growth rings. The similarity in structure between dinosaur and mammal bone was regarded as further evidence that dinosaurs were 'warm-blooded' like mammals. However, more recently it has been shown that 'cold-blooded' turtles and crocodiles also have bones with lots of canals in them and small mammals and birds have solid bone. It now seems that lots of canals in bones may be associated with rapid growth and large size of animals rather than strictly with 'warm-' or 'cold-bloodedness'.

Present opinions

Today it is generally agreed that, although we may never be able to prove it, small, agile dinosaurs such as *Deinonychus*, *Ornithomimus* and *Hypsilophodon* (see pages 52–9) may well have been *endothermic*, somewhat like modern mammals. However, for the vast majority of dinosaurs *endothermy* may well have been unnecessary! Work done on alligators in the 1940s has shown that big alligators show much less change than small ones. That is, the larger you are the less your body temperature changes. Applying this principle to dinosaurs (most of which are very large — far larger than alligators), it seems likely that their body temperature would change hardly at all between day and night. Thus many dinosaurs would have been 'warm-blooded' not because they were *endotherms* but simply because they were enormously large.

Postscript

It is a curious fact that over the past few years we have learned a great deal about the temperature regulation of many *living* animals *only* because of interest in the controversy of 'warm-bloodedness' in long extinct dinosaurs.

Glossary

Adapt: change to make more suitable.

Alkaloid: poisonous substance produced by some flowering plants.

Amphibian: animal which lays soft, jelly-covered eggs in water, where its young develop first as tadpoles. Modern amphibians (frogs, toads, newts and salamanders) have a soft moist skin.

Anapsids: groups of the most primitive reptiles, to which the turtles and tortoises seem to belong. No opening in the skull behind the eye (see *Hylonomus*, pages 18–19).

Anatomist: one who studies the structure of animal bodies.

Ankylosaur: heavily armoured plant-eating ornithischian dinosaur of the Jurassic and Cretaceous. Some had a large tail club which they used as a defensive weapon (pages 68–69).

Archosaurs: a group of reptiles including crocodiles, pterosaurs, ornithischian and saurischian dinosaurs.

Carnosaur: meat-eating bipedal saurischian dinosaur, generally heavily built, with short neck and arms, powerful legs and enormous head (pages 38–39, 56–58).

Ceratopian: horned ornithischian dinosaur of the Late Cretaceous, of which *Triceratops* is a famous example (pages 66–67).

Coelurosaur: meat-eating bipedal saurischian dinosaur, generally lightly built, with long neck and arms, slender legs and relatively small head (pages 30–39).

Cynodont: very mammal-like reptile of the Permian and Triassic periods, many of which were rather dog-like in appearance; some ate meat, others plants (pages 24–26).

Diapsids: reptiles with two openings in the skull behind the eye. There are two major types: lepidosaurs (lizards and snakes) and archosaurs (dinosaurs, crocodiles and their relatives) (pages 20–25).

Dicynodont: peculiar plant-eating, mammal-like reptile common in Permian and Triassic times. Most of them had only two large tusk-like teeth in the upper jaw (pages 24, 26).

Digest: break down (food) into small particles, or molecules, which can be absorbed into the body.

Dinosaur: popular name for the two groups of archosaur reptile: the Ornithischia and Saurischia, both of which were dominant in the Mesozoic Era.

Erosion: process of wearing away. Used here to describe the wearing away of rocks by climatic effects.

**Right:
A Plesiosaur**

Euryapsids: extinct group of aquatic reptiles including the plesiosaurs and ichthyosaurs, nothosaurs and placodonts, characterized by a single (upper) opening in the side of the skull behind the eye (pages 34–35, 70–71).

Evolve: develop gradually and naturally. Used here in the sense that over many generations a species may change in a way which makes it better suited to the changing environment in which it lives.

Extinct: having come to an end, died out.

Geologist: one who studies the rocks of the Earth's crust.

Hadrosaur: moderately large herbivorous ornithischian dinosaur of the Late Cretaceous. Often called 'duck-billed' dinosaur because of the flattened duck-like beak. Some had extraordinary crests on their heads (pages 60–61, 65).

Ichthyosaur: aquatic reptile of the Mesozoic Era. Remarkable for streamlined shape and resemblance to modern dolphins (pages 34–5, 70–71).

Mammal: animal which has warm blood and hairy skin and grows only two sets of teeth: a milk set and a permanent set. The female usually gives birth to live young, which it suckles on mother's milk (pages 19–25).

Mesozoic Era: the period of time in Earth's history between 225 and 65 million years ago (the Triassic, Jurassic and Cretaceous Periods) when reptiles ruled the land (pages 12–13).

Mosasaur: large flesh-eating aquatic relative of the present-day lizards. It lived in Late Cretaceous times (pages 70–71).

Nostril: opening of the nose.

Nothosaur: aquatic reptile of the Triassic Period, slightly lizard-like in shape, probably a relative of the plesiosaurs (pages 34–5).

Nutrition: nourishment, food.

Ornithischian: dinosaur characterized by an arrangement of the hip bones similar to that in birds.

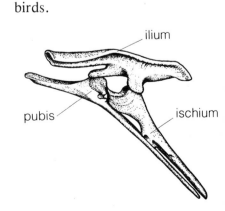

76

hycephalosaur: medium-sized
thischian dinosaur notable
its extraordinarily thick bony
1. Lived in Cretaceous times
es 21, 62–63).

eontologist: one who studies
of the geological past.

ycosaur: primitive member of the
apsid group of reptiles; some are
ed 'sail-back'. Lived in Late
boniferous and Early Permian
es (pages 18–19).

Triassic Period, ancestor to later
groups of archosaurs (crocodiles,
dinosaurs, and perhaps pterosaurs).
Pterosaur: flying reptile of the
Mesozoic Era, somewhat bat-like in
appearance (pages 34–35, 70–71).
Reptile: a scaly-skinned animal
which generally lays eggs with shells
and is cold-blooded (pages 18–21).
Rhynchosaur: peculiar plant-eating
reptile of the Triassic Period with
unusual beak-like jaws (pages
24, 26).

Skull: bony part of the head which
encloses the brain and sense organs.
Species: group of similar animals or
plants which breed with each other
to produce fertile offspring, but not
with any other organism.
Synapsids: extinct group of reptiles
ancestral to the mammals and
characterized by a single (lower)
opening in the side of the skull
behind the eye (pages 18–21).
Therapsids: descendants of the
pelycosaurs, these synapsid reptiles
resemble mammals in many ways.
Particularly abundant from Middle
Permian until Middle Triassic times.

ove: *Dimetrodon*, an example of
ail back'.

codont: rather turtle-like aquatic
tile of the Triassic Period. Many
large, flat, crushing teeth for
ding on shellfish (pages 34–35).

teosaur: reptile of the early
up of saurischian dinosaurs
ed prosauropods, *Plateosaurus*
ng its Latin name (pages 28–31).

siosaur: large-bodied, aquatic
tile of the Mesozoic Era, which
m using large paddle-like legs
ges 70–71).

dator: one who lives by feeding
eying) on others.

oterosuchian': early, heavily
lt archosaur of the Late Permian
l Early Triassic.

eudosuchian': rather slenderly
lt, active archosaur of the

Saurischian: dinosaur characterized
by an arrangement of the hip bones
similar to that of lizards.

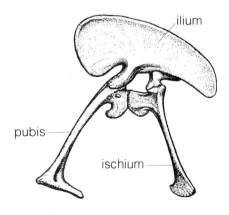

Sauropod: enormous, plant-eating,
quadrupedal saurischian dinosaurs.
Apatosaurus is a famous example
(pages 28, 37, 39–43, 47).
Serrated: notched like the edge of a
saw.

Above: *Cynognathus*, a therapsid
(see pages 22, 23). *Cynognathus*
lived about 220 million years ago.
It was about as big as a pig and
probably came from the same line
of ancestry as the mammals. It was
an active predator, with teeth
capable of biting, stabbing and
chewing like those of living
mammals.

Dinosaur names

Allosaurus (ALLoh-SAWrus): different reptile.

Anchisaurus (ANki-SAWrus): near reptile.

Ankylosaurus (ANkiloh-SAWrus): stiff reptile.

Apatosaurus (ay-PATToh-SAWrus): deceptive reptile.

Archaeopteryx (ARki-OPterriks): ancient wing.

Askeptosaurus (assKEPtoh-SAWrus): reptile too small to be seen, or unseen reptile.

Brachiosaurus (BRAKKi-oh-SAWrus): arm reptile.

Brontosaurus (BRONtoh-SAWrus): thunder reptile.

Camptosaurus (KAMPtoh-SAWrus): bent reptile.

Centrosaurus (SEN-TROW-SAWrus); sharp point reptile.

Cephalaspis (KEFFal-ASSpis): head shield.

Chasmosaurus (KAZmoh-SAWrus): ravine reptile.

Coelophysis (SEEloh-FYsis): hollow form

Coelurus (see-LOOR-us): hollow tail.

Above: *Archaeopteryx*, the earliest known bird, a perfect intermediate between reptiles and birds. See pages 8, 13, 20, 36, 37, 50–1.

Compsognathus (KOMPsoh-GNAYthus): pretty jaw.

Corythosaurus (KORRIthoh-SAWrus): helmet reptile.

Cynognathus (SYnoh-GNAYthus): dog jaw.

Deinonychus (dye-NONNy-kus): terrible claw.

Dimetrodon (dye-METrohdon): two-sized tooth.

Dimorphodon (dye-MORFohdon): two-formed tooth.

Diplodocus (DIPloh-DOHkus): double beam.

Dryosaurus (DRY-oh-SAWrus): wood reptile, or oak reptile.

Edmontosaurus (edMONtoh-SAWrus): reptile from Edmonton (Canada).

Elasmosaurus (eLAZmoh-SAWrus): plate reptile.

Euoplocephalus (you-OPloe-KEFFalus): well-armoured head.

Euparkeria (you-park-EERia): Parker's true reptile.

Eusthenopteron (youss-then-OPterron): true strong oar.

Heterodontosaurus (HETTeroh-DONToh-SAWrus): different-toothed reptile.

Hylonomus (HYloh-NOHmus): wood mouse.

Hypsilophodon (HIPPsi-LOHFohdon): high-ridge tooth.

Ichthyosaurus (IKthi-oh-SAWrus): fish reptile.

Ichthyostega (IKthi-oh-STEEGa): fish roof.

Iguanodon (i-GWAHnoe-don): iguana tooth.

Kritosaurus (KRITToh-SAWrus): chosen reptile.

Lesothosaurus (leSOO-toh-SAWrus): reptile from Lesotho.

Lycaenops (ly-KAY-nops): wolf face.

Mandasuchus (MANda-SOO-kus): crocodile from the Manda Formation (Tanzania).

Massospondylus (MASSoh-SPONdillus): big vertebra.

Megalosaurus (MEGGa-loh-SAWrus: great reptile.

Megazostrodon (MEGGa-ZOStrohdon): big-girdle tooth.

Mixosaurus (Mis-oh-SawRus): h⟨ reptile.

Mosasaurus (MOHZa-SAWrus): reptile from the Meuse.

Ophiacodon (OHfi-AKohdon): snake-like tooth.

Ornithomimus (ORNithoh-MEEMus): bird imitator.

Ouranosaurus (oo-RAHNoh-SAWrus): valiant monitor lizard.

Pachycephalosaurus (PAKKi-SEFFaloe-SAWrus): thick-head⟨ reptile.

Pachyrhinosaurus (PAKKi-RYEnoh-SAWrus): thick-nosed reptile.

Parasaurolophus (PARRa-Saw-ROLLoe-fuss): rather like a ridg⟨ reptile.

Plateosaurus (PLATTi-oh-SAWrus): flat reptile.

Protoceratops (PROHtoh-SERRatops): first horned face.

Psittacosaurus (Sit-TAKKoh-SAWrus): parrot reptile.

Pteranodon (ter-RANNoh-don): winged and toothless.

Pterodactylus (TERRoh-DACTillus): finger wing.

Quetzalcoatlus (Kwetzal-CO-Atl⟨ legendary or mythical bird.

Rhamphorynchus (RAMfoe-RINkus): beak snout.

Scelidosaurus (Skel-LYdoh-SAWrus): limb reptile.

Stegoceras (Steg-GOSSerus): roo⟨ horn.

Stegosaurus (STEGoh-SAWrus): roof reptile.

Stenaulorhynchus (Sten-AWLon-SAWrus): narrow, flute beak.

Tenontosaurus (Ten-ONtoh-SAWrus): sinew lizard.

Thrinaxodon (thrin-AXoh-don): trident tooth.

Triceratops (Try-KERRatops): three-horned face.

Tyrannosaurus (ty-RANNoh-SAWRus): tyrant reptile.

Pictures: Courtesy of American Museum of Natural History 64; Dr. D. Norman 9TR, CR, BR; Bayerische Staatssammlung für Paläontologie und historische Geologie München 37R; K. A. & G. Beckett 9TL; Courtesy of the Trustees of the British Museum (Natural History) 10, 11L, 60, 69; Bruce Zeffa 62–3; Zofia Kielan-Jaworowska 65; Pat Morris 9BL, 11R, 14R, 35; Museum für Naturkunde, Berlin 6L, 8; Natural Science Photos/Dick Brown 6–7; Hal Williams, Brigham Young University Public Communications 41.